Bloom's
GUIDES

Joseph Conrad's
Heart of Darkness

The Adventures of
  Huckleberry Finn
All the Pretty Horses
Animal Farm
The Autobiography of Malcolm X
The Awakening
The Bell Jar
Beloved
Beowulf
Brave New World
The Canterbury Tales
Catch-22
The Catcher in the Rye
The Chosen
The Crucible
Cry, the Beloved Country
Death of a Salesman
Fahrenheit 451
Frankenstein
The Glass Menagerie
The Grapes of Wrath
Great Expectations
The Great Gatsby
Hamlet
The Handmaid's Tale
Heart of Darkness
The House on Mango Street
I Know Why the Caged Bird Sings
The Iliad
Invisible Man
Jane Eyre

The Kite Runner
Lord of the Flies
Macbeth
Maggie: A Girl of the Streets
The Member of the Wedding
The Metamorphosis
Native Son
Night
1984
The Odyssey
Oedipus Rex
Of Mice and Men
One Hundred Years of Solitude
Pride and Prejudice
Ragtime
A Raisin in the Sun
The Red Badge of Courage
Romeo and Juliet
The Scarlet Letter
A Separate Peace
Slaughterhouse-Five
Snow Falling on Cedars
The Stranger
A Streetcar Named Desire
The Sun Also Rises
A Tale of Two Cities
The Things They Carried
To Kill a Mockingbird
Uncle Tom's Cabin
The Waste Land
Wuthering Heights

Bloom's
GUIDES

Joseph Conrad's
Heart of Darkness

Edited & with an Introduction
by Harold Bloom

BLOOM'S
LITERARY CRITICISM
An imprint of Infobase Publishing

Bloom's Guides: Heart of Darkness

Copyright © 2009 by Infobase Publishing

Introduction © 2009 by Harold Bloom

All rights reserved. No part of this book may be reproduced or utilized in any form or by any means, electronic or mechanical, including photocopying, recording, or by any information storage or retrieval systems, without permission in writing from the publisher. For information contact:

Bloom's Literary Criticism
An imprint of Infobase Publishing
132 West 31st Street
New York, NY 10001

Library of Congress Cataloging-in-Publication Data
Heart of darkness / edited and with an introduction by Harold Bloom.
    p. cm. — (Bloom's guides)
    Includes bibliographical references (p.) and index.
    ISBN 978-1-60413-200-7
    1. Conrad, Joseph, 1857–1924. Heart of darkness. 2. Psychological fiction, English—History and criticism. 3. Africa—In literature. I. Bloom, Harold.
    PR6005.O4H4767 2008
    823'.912—dc22

2008037128

Bloom's Literary Criticism books are available at special discounts when purchased in bulk quantities for businesses, associations, institutions, or sales promotions. Please call our Special Sales Department in New York at (212) 967-8800 or (800) 322-8755.

You can find Bloom's Literary Criticism on the World Wide Web at
http://www.chelseahouse.com

Contributing Editor: Jennifer Banach Palladino
Cover design by Takeshi Takahashi
Printed in the United States of America
Bang EJB 10 9 8 7 6 5 4 3 2 1
This book is printed on acid-free paper.

All links and Web addresses were checked and verified to be correct at the time of publication. Because of the dynamic nature of the Web, some addresses and links may have changed since publication and may no longer be valid.

Contents

Introduction

HAROLD BLOOM

I

In Conrad's "Youth" (1898), Marlow gives us a brilliant description of the sinking of the *Judea:*

"Between the darkness of earth and heaven she was burning fiercely upon a disc of purple sea shot by the blood-red play of gleams; upon a disc of water glittering and sinister. A high, clear flame, an immense and lonely flame, ascended from the ocean, and from its summit the black smoke poured continuously at the sky. She burned furiously; mournful and imposing like a funeral pile kindled in the night, surrounded by the sea, watched over by the stars. A magnificent death had come like a grace, like a gift, like a reward to that old ship at the end of her laborious day. The surrender of her weary ghost to the keeper of the stars and sea was stirring like the sight of a glorious triumph. The masts fell just before daybreak, and for a moment there was a burst and turmoil of sparks that seemed to fill with flying fire the night patient and watchful, the vast night lying silent upon the sea. At daylight she was only a charred shell, floating still under a cloud of smoke and bearing a glowing mass of coal within."

"Then the oars were got out, and the boats forming in a line moved around her remains as if in procession—the longboat leading. As we pulled across her stern a slim dart of fire shot out viciously at us, and suddenly she went down, head first, in a great hiss of steam. The unconsumed stern was the last to sink; but the paint had gone, had cracked, had peeled off, and there were no letters, there was no word, no stubborn device that was like her soul, to flash at the rising sun her creed and her name."

The apocalyptic vividness is enhanced by the visual namelessness of the "unconsumed stern," as though the creed of Christ's people maintained both its traditional refusal to violate the Second Commandment and its traditional affirmation of its not-to-be-named God. With the *Judea*, Conrad sinks the romance of youth's illusions, but like all losses in Conrad this submersion in the destructive element is curiously dialectical, since only experiential loss allows for the compensation of an imaginative gain in the representation of artistic truth. Originally the ephebe of Flaubert and of Flaubert's "son," Maupassant, Conrad was reborn as the narrative disciple of Henry James, the James of *The Spoils of Poynton* and *What Maisie Knew*, rather than the James of the final phase.

Ian Watt convincingly traces the genesis of Marlow to the way that "James developed the indirect narrative approach through the sensitive central intelligence of one of the characters." Marlow, whom James derided as "that preposterous magic mariner," actually represents Conrad's swerve away from the excessive strength of James's influence on him. By always "mixing himself up with the narrative," in James's words, Marlow guarantees an enigmatic reserve that increases the distance between the impressionistic techniques of Conrad and James. Though there is little valid comparison that can be made between Conrad's greatest achievements and the hesitant, barely fictional status of Pater's *Marius the Epicurean*, Conrad's impressionism is as extreme and solipsistic as Pater's. There is a definite parallel between the fates of Sebastian Van Storck (in Pater's *Imaginary Portraits*) and Decoud in *Nostromo*.

In his 1897 "Preface" to *The Nigger of the "Narcissus,"* Conrad famously insisted that his creative task was "before all to make you *see*." He presumably was aware that he thus joined himself to a line of prose seers whose latest representatives were Carlyle, Ruskin, and Pater. There is a movement in that group from Carlyle's exuberant "Natural Supernaturalism" through Ruskin's paganization of evangelical fervor to Pater's evasive and skeptical epicurean materialism, with its eloquent suggestion that all we can see is the flux of sensations. Conrad exceeds Pater in the reduction of impressionism to a state of consciousness where the seeing narrator is hopelessly mixed up with the seen narrative. James may seem an impressionist when compared to Flaubert, but alongside Conrad he is clearly shown to be a kind of Platonist, imposing forms and resolutions on the flux of human relations by an exquisite formal geometry altogether his own.

To observe that Conrad is metaphysically less of an idealist is hardly to argue that he is necessarily a stronger novelist than his master, James. It may suggest though that Conrad's originality is more disturbing than that of James, and may help explain why Conrad, rather than James, became the dominant influence on the generation of American novelists that included Hemingway, Fitzgerald, and Faulkner. The cosmos of *The Sun Also Rises*, *The Great Gatsby*, and *As I Lay Dying* derives from *Heart of Darkness* and *Nostromo* rather than from *The Ambassadors* and *The Golden Bowl*. Darl Bundren is the extreme inheritor of Conrad's quest to carry impressionism into its heart of darkness in the human awareness that we are only a flux of sensations gazing outward on a flux of impressions.

II

Heart of Darkness may always be a critical battleground between readers who regard it as an aesthetic triumph, and those like myself who doubt its ability to rescue us from its own hopeless obscurantism. That Marlow seems, at moments, not to know what he is talking about, is almost certainly one of the narrative's deliberate strengths, but if Conrad also seems finally not to know, then he necessarily loses some of his authority as a storyteller. Perhaps he loses it to death—our death, or our anxiety that he will not sustain the illusion of his fiction's duration long enough for us to sublimate the frustrations it brings us.

These frustrations need not be deprecated. Conrad's diction, normally flawless, is notoriously vague throughout *Heart of Darkness*. E.M. Forster's wicked comment on Conrad's entire work is justified perhaps only when applied to *Heart of Darkness*:

Misty in the middle as well as at the edges, the secret cask of his genius contains a vapour rather than a jewel. . . . No creed, in fact.

Forster's misty vapor seems to inhabit such Conradian recurrent modifiers as "monstrous," "unspeakable," "atrocious," and many more, but these are minor defects compared to the involuntary self-parody that Conrad inflicts on himself. There are moments that sound more like James Thurber lovingly satirizing Conrad than like Conrad:

> We had carried Kurtz into the pilot house: there was more air there. Lying on the couch, he stared through the open shutter. There was an eddy in the mass of human bodies, and the woman with helmeted head and tawny cheeks rushed out to the very brink of the stream. She put out her hands, shouted something, and all that wild mob took up the shout in a roaring chorus of articulated, rapid, breathless utterance.
> "Do you understand this?" I asked.
> He kept on looking out past me with fiery, longing eyes, with a mingled expression of wistfulness and hate. He made no answer, but I saw a smile, a smile of indefinable meaning, appear on his colorless lips that a moment after twitched convulsively. "Do I not?" he said slowly, gasping, as if the words had been torn out of him by a supernatural power.

This cannot be defended as an instance of what Frank Kermode calls a language "needed when Marlow is not equal to the experience described." Has the experience been described here? Smiles of "indefinable meaning" are smiled once too often in a literary text if they are smiled even once. *Heart of Darkness* has taken on some of the power of myth, even if the book is limited by its involuntary obscurantism. It has haunted American literature from T.S. Eliot's poetry through our major novelists of the era 1920 to 1940, on to a line of movies that go from *Citizen Kane* of Orson Welles (a substitute for an abandoned Welles project to film *Heart of Darkness*) on to Coppola's *Apocalypse Now*. In this instance, Conrad's formlessness seems to have worked as an aid, so diffusing his conception as to have made it available to an almost universal audience.

Biographical Sketch

Joseph Conrad was born Józef Teodor Konrad Nalecz Korzeniowski on December 3, 1857, near Berdichev in the Ukraine, a region that had once been part of Poland but was then ruled by Russia. His parents, Apollo and Evelina Bobrowski Korzeniowski, belonged to the educated landowning Polish gentry and fought for Polish independence. In 1862, Apollo Korzeniowski, a talented writer and translator, was exiled to Vologda in northern Russia. The difficult life there took its toll on the family, and Conrad's mother died in 1865 and his father in 1869. Conrad moved to Kraków to live with his maternal uncle. He spent much of his time reading Charles Dickens and Victor Hugo but also dreamed of the life of a sailor.

In October 1874, Conrad received his uncle's permission to enter the French merchant marine. While learning seamanship in Marseille, he led a wild life full of romantic adventures and reckless spending. He made three voyages to the West Indies and in his spare time engaged in gunrunning for the Carlist faction in Spain. In 1878, he shot himself (although he claimed he had been wounded in a duel). After recovering and settling his debts with his uncle's help, he left Marseille on the English frigate *Mavis*.

Knowing just a few words of English, Conrad joined the English merchant navy.

Over the next sixteen years, he prospered as a seaman, visiting ports in Australia, South America, India, Borneo, and the South Pacific, among other places. In 1886, he achieved several important milestones: he was made the master of his own ship, became a British subject, and changed his name to Joseph Conrad. Traveling to Africa in 1890, he ventured up the Congo River with the Belgian colonial service. There he contracted malaria, which plagued him for years.

As a result of ill health and his growing interest in writing, Conrad retired from his seafaring career in 1894 and settled permanently in England. A year later, he published his first novel, *Almayer's Folly*. The story, based on a Dutch trader Conrad had known in Borneo, garnered praise from such luminaries as H.G. Wells and Henry James. Conrad became friends with many of the leading writers of his day and even collaborated with Ford Madox Ford on two novels, *The Inheritors* (1901) and *Romance* (1903). In 1896, he published *An Outcast of the Islands*, also set in Borneo, and married Jessie George, with whom he had two sons. During the next two years, he published *The Nigger of the "Narcissus,"* which employed poetic realism to describe the negative effects of one man on a ship's crew, and *Tales of Unrest.*

Although he struggled financially and was racked with self-doubt about his creative ability, Conrad produced books of remarkable artistry, infusing adventure stories with profound explorations of the conflicts between and within men. His masterful novel *Lord Jim* (1900), which was inspired by a story he heard of a crew's desertion, brilliantly illustrates the plight of a man who had imagined himself a hero but fails when tested by dangerous circumstances; the man then devotes his life to trying to appease his conscience and recover his honor. In addition to the novel *Typhoon*, in 1902 he published the collection *Youth*, which contained *The End of the Tether* and *Heart of Darkness* (first published in *Blackwood's Edinburgh Magazine* in February, March, and April 1899) as well as the title story.

At this time, Conrad shifted his focus from the stirring forces at sea to the turbulence of politics. With *Nostromo* (1904), he created a fictional South American country to illustrate the frustrating futility of man's efforts at change. *The Secret Agent* (1907) describes an anarchist bomb plot in London. *Under Western Eyes* (1911) depicts the Russian aristocracy in a tale of betrayal and a search for redemption.

Conrad remained prolific until the end of his life. He published autobiographical reminiscences in *The Mirror of the Sea* (1906) and *A Personal Record* (1912). The stories "The Secret Sharer" (first published in *Harper's Monthly Magazine* in August and September 1910 and included in *'Twixt Land and Sea*, 1912) and *The Shadow-Line* (1917) were also semiautobiographical. In

1913, Conrad finally achieved popular success in England and the United States with *Chance;* after years of critical acclaim, he at last secured a measure of financial security and fame. He followed this with *Victory* (1915), *The Arrow of Gold* (1919), and *The Rescue* (1920). His last novel, *The Rover* (1923), was a French Revolution drama and his final work, *Last Essays,* was a nonfiction collection published posthumously in 1926. Conrad died on August 3, 1924, at Bishopsbourne, Kent. He is now recognized as one of the great British novelists and short story writers of his time.

The Story Behind the Story

In 1890, at thirty-one years of age, Joseph Conrad set off for Africa, where he was to command a riverboat on the Congo River, a waterway that flowed through the very region the author had dreamed of exploring since he was a young boy. As the orphaned son of exiled Polish revolutionaries, Conrad had committed himself to a life at sea at an early age and had traveled extensively, but there is no doubt that he must have had high expectations for this long-awaited voyage in particular. Rather than fulfill Conrad's childhood fantasies of adventure and glory in conquest, the trip revealed harsh realities that would have a life-altering effect on the author. Conrad spent two months as a first mate and commanded the ship only for a brief period of time when the captain fell ill. After reaching the location where he was to take command of his own ship, it was revealed that the boat was damaged, and Conrad had to travel under other leadership once again. Certainly more disconcerting than the surrounding presence and subsequent threat of physical illness and the disappointment of being unable to assume his post as captain was Conrad's exposure to those most disturbing elements of humanity witnessed in the Congo. He was greeted by an overwhelming exhibition of greed, violence, and, arguably, evil, which revealed itself in the entrenched imperialist activity in the region. Conrad reportedly returned to England ill and disillusioned.

Although Conrad did not begin to write *Heart of Darkness* until approximately eight years after his return to England, it was this trip and the diary he kept during his travels in the Congo that would serve as the major sources of inspiration for Charlie Marlow's own tale, as recounted in the novella. Readers, scholars, and critics had no trouble pinpointing the many similarities between the story's primary narrator, Marlow, and Conrad himself. Additionally, scholars and critics noted similarities between Kurtz and Georges-Antoine Klein, a sick agent picked up by Conrad's boat who did not survive the return voyage. Upon further consideration, congruencies were also evident between Kurtz and numerous other personalities of the day including the infamous Welsh explorer Henry Morton Stanley. Conrad was quick to acknowledge that *Heart of Darkness* did indeed have its basis in reality.

The story opens with an image of London as it was in Conrad's day—the wealthiest and most powerful city in the world—and addressed one of the most important social issues of the era. England had begun extending its domain via imperialism, an activity that Belgium's King Leopold was thoroughly exploiting in the Congo region under the guise of civilizing missions and international trade. Through Marlow's tale, readers were made aware of the horrific aspects of imperialism and colonialism that may have been previously undisclosed to the public, or which had at least gone generally unacknowledged and uncontested.

Readers quickly found, however, that imperialism was not the sole subject of the novella, nor were its concerns necessarily bound up in a particular moment in time. Conrad also exposed significantly deeper, universal issues of humanity and civilization. Scholars began to warn of the danger in oversimplifying *Heart of Darkness* by reducing themes and focusing on limited readings and narrow interpretations. With this in mind, it is important to remember that the experiences represented in *Heart of Darkness* do not simply stem from historical concerns related to Conrad's time in the Congo but from the sum of his experiences, including the events of his own personal history. The death of his parents following their exile from Poland no doubt influenced Conrad's view of politics and social issues, and many scholars and critics have speculated that the author's estrangement from his own country played a large part in the successful reception of *Heart of Darkness* by a global audience.

While *Heart of Darkness* is commonly recalled in its novella form as published in 1902 in Conrad's *Youth and Other Stories*, the story actually appeared as a three-part series in *Blackwood's Edinburgh Magazine* a few years earlier, marking a new period in the author's career. It exhibited a unique capacity for straddling the boundaries of literature, evidencing characteristics of many different periods. The story contained elements of the popular heroism evident in Victorian works, and its focus on imagination and those deeper, emotional aspects of the human experience aligned it with the romantic tradition. But the novella was also strikingly modern, dabbling in frame narratives and covert plots and utilizing multiple narrators and achronological timeframes. Many scholars would come to argue that it was the seminal work in the emergence of modernist literature.

Discussion of the novella gained significant momentum in the 1950s and 1960s, peaking in the late 1970s, as the work came under fire when novelist Chinua Achebe alleged that Conrad was simply and undeniably a racist. While many scholars came to the author's defense, Conrad was also criticized heavily by feminists during this time for his depiction of women. Furthermore, critics began speculating about Conrad's insistence on the unnamable and the mysterious. This prominent characteristic of Conrad's work was considered by many to be a failure of language and thereby a failure of the author, certainly a flaw not befitting one of the major novelists of all time. Yet, it has been pointed out, it is perhaps the author's unique propensity for ambiguity that has opened the work to a wide range of critical interpretations. It is certainly this flexibility that has driven the success of *Heart of Darkness* and will, no doubt, continue to propel further study in the future. Despite the passage of time and ongoing controversies surrounding the work, *Heart of Darkness* has had a striking influence on writers, artists, and thinkers from all over the globe. Constant, varied critical interpretation and discussion of the work have allowed it to remain highly visible at the surface of the literary canon. The novella remains immensely popular—and controversial—in contemporary times and is now recognized as the most studied work of literature in college and university curricula.

List of Characters

Charlie Marlow is the protagonist and central narrative voice of *Heart of Darkness*. He delivers his entire narrative on the *Nellie* sitting in a Buddha-like posture, implying enlightenment or perpetual meditation. Naturally curious, idealistically judgmental, or rather too naively self-assured, Marlow joins "the trading society" as a steamboat skipper. His journey into the interior of the jungle symbolizes the internal exploration of his own moral integrity. Kurtz, with whom Marlow almost immediately identifies and who is the supposed embodiment of his moral ideals, awaits him at the heart of darkness. Marlow's refusal to lie represents his own ethical integrity: "You know I hate, detest, and can't bear a lie, not because I am straighter than the rest of us, but simply because it appalls me." Yet, as he proceeds from one station to the next and continues up the river, gradually beginning to internalize the disenchanting corruption of his surroundings, he moves closer and closer to telling lies of his own. The confrontation with Kurtz marks Marlow's final debilitating recognition of the inadequacy of his personal morals to influence or command circumstances beyond his comprehension and control. Thereafter, it becomes easier and easier for him to lie.

Kurtz's presence in most of *Heart of Darkness* is primarily through the words of other people—a fitting characterization, as he turns out to be an individual barely more tangible than his disembodied voice. The fact that he is half English and half French encourages the denigrating ideas about his character that the manager, an Englishman, conceives. Kurtz is the chief of the Inner Station and is described as magnetically charming with an incredible faculty for articulated expression. Although he is childishly selfish, materialistic, deluded, and mentally unstable when Marlow meets him, Conrad infers that he was once a principled man of substance, driven to the wilderness by his ambition to fulfill "immense plans." In the end, he seems to regain himself, dying in a "supreme moment of complete knowledge" and moral possession of his soul.

Summary and Analysis

Heart of Darkness begins on the Thames River with a scene peacefully unremarkable except for the dark air "brooding . . . over the biggest, and the greatest, town on earth." The first significant association of darkness to civilization is established in these preliminary passages, in addition to introducing the outer framework of the narrative. Anchored and waiting to set sail is the *Nellie*, on which the outer narrative takes place. Aboard the *Nellie* are five acquaintances who share "the bond of the sea." There is the captain—actually a director of companies—a lawyer, an accountant, Marlow, and the narrator. As they wait for the tide to turn, the brilliance of the end of the day is noted and contrasted with the "gloom brooding over a crowd of men." Musing on the view of the Thames, the narrator recollects the men who have previously sailed it, "the men of whom the nation is proud," citing as examples Sir Francis Drake and Sir John Franklin, a revealing statement about the nation's temperament: although both Drake and Franklin were knights in name, Drake was known for being little more than a pirate, while Franklin, who never returned from his expedition, was driven by similar material interests. The sun sets, and the Thames is lit by "a great stir of [ships'] lights." Yet again, the "brooding gloom" hanging over what is now referred to as "the monstrous town" is mentioned, and Marlow recalls that it, also, was once "one of the dark places of the earth." Evoking images of the wilderness, marshes, and forests and of the brutality of prehistoric human life, Marlow draws a subtle parallel between Roman imperialism and English colonialism but differentiates sheer "robbery with violence" from "conquest of the earth" redeemed by "an idea at the back of it."

This parallel inspires Marlow to begin a tale about one of his "inconclusive experiences" and marks a relationship between the central narrative on the Thames and the following inner narrative on the river to the heart of darkness. Back in London, after a few years on the eastern seas, Marlow is wandering about, looking for something to occupy his time. A map he

19

notices in a shop window reminds him of the blank white spaces that in his boyhood years represented unexplored regions. The largest one, which had most excited his imagination, has since been filled with the names of cities, rivers, and lakes and "had become a place of darkness." Still, he is fascinated by a snakelike river winding through the continent, and using the influences of an aunt, secures a position as a steamboat skipper with "a big concern, a company for trade on that river." The position becomes available through portentous circumstances: Marlow's predecessor, Fresleven, "the gentlest, quietest creature," beats a village chief and is hanged for it.

Marlow's visit to the company's headquarters is no more promising. The headquarters are silent and deserted, he is greeted by two tacit women knitting black wool (reminiscent of the Fates weaving), and there is the uncomfortable ceremony of having to sign a contract. In addition, a clerk who enthuses about the company's glorious business, which is, ironically, "to run an oversea empire, and make no end of coin by trade," conversely alludes to the foolishness of the adventurers "out there," as does a company doctor who nonchalantly asks if there is any history of mental illness in Marlow's family. During a meeting with his aunt before his departure, Marlow hears more about glory and being "an emissary of light" and "weaning those ignorant millions from their horrid ways." His awkward hint to her that the company is not embarking on a noble enterprise but a mercenary one, is brushed aside. Further characterizations of the company's mission inaugurate Marlow into the "high and just proceedings" of colonialism. He departs Europe on a French steamer that, sailing along the coast of Africa, at one point delivers mail to a man of war, "incomprehenibl[y], firing into a continent," at a supposed "enemy" camp of native residents. Arriving at his first camp, he is met by six black men chained together, "raw matter" behind which "one of the reclaimed, the product of new forces at work, strolled despondently."

Integral to and indicative of Marlow's ensuing internal transitions is a slight shift from common perspectives of light and dark. Sunshine in this land is more than once portrayed as "blinding." Light has become a destructive element. To escape from the sun and the indirect, silent accusation of the chained men, Marlow steps into the shade of some trees and discovers a mass of black shapes, the concentrates of human misery wrung out by the "philanthropic" work going on: "pain, abandonment and despair, . . . disease and starvation." As he hastens away, Marlow encounters the white-clad vision of the company's chief accountant, from whom he will initially hear the name *Kurtz*. The accountant is the first in a series of personages who are as thin as their appearances. The accountant's physical presence, likened to that of "a hairdresser's dummy," is marked by Marlow to give no indication of the "great demoralization of the land" around him.

Ten days later a caravan arrives, and, with it, Marlow departs for Central Station. His only white traveling companion is "rather too fleshy," constantly faints, and eventually contracts a fever, which inspires no sympathy in Marlow but rather annoyance to the point that he asks the man what he is doing in Africa given his delicate makeup. This unconscious partiality toward survival of nature's physically fittest is the first sign of Marlow's ultimate compliance with the "efficiency" of social Darwinism, the survival of the socially fittest, and the "redeeming idea" behind his entire experience. He eventually arrives at Central Station, only to discover that the steamer of which he is supposedly the skipper sunk a few days previous. A mustached man attempts to reassure Marlow by saying "Everyone had behaved splendidly." Meeting the manager, Marlow remarks that such an ordinary man must have achieved and maintained his position merely by never getting ill. Affirming that "men who come out here should have no entrails," the manager also equates himself with the accountant as one of Joseph Conrad's "hollow men." Marlow's speculation that "perhaps there was nothing within him" refers more to the manager's moral emptiness that to his physical state. Frustrated and mildly disgusted, Marlow sets to work rescuing his steamboat. Trying to separate himself from those colonists whose worship of ivory is no more "glorious" than the Romans' manifestation of brute strength, he rejects the affected reality of the station and finds in work, which those at the station view as mere show, the opportunity to discover himself and his own reality.

After a fire at Central Station, during which the mustached man is heard again to comment that "everyone is behaving splendidly," as he rushes around filling a leaking pail with water, Marlow meets the manager's assistant, whom he overhears ominously mentioning Kurtz. This "papier-mâché Mephistopheles . . . [with] nothing inside but a little loose dirt," whose function for the past year has supposedly been to make bricks, although there is none in sight at Central Station, supplies Marlow with more details of Kurtz, the chief of the Inner Station: "He is an emissary of pity, and science, and progress . . . higher intelligence, wide sympathies, a singleness of purpose." This resemblance to Marlow's roles as an "emissary of light" offers him something he can morally respect, someone perhaps akin to himself; however, this psychological affinity anticipates that Kurtz's moral corruption will precede Marlow's own final compromise of ideals. As the manager's assistant drones on, Marlow marvels at "the silence of the land, the amazing reality of its concealed life," so bluntly in contrast to the unreality surrounding Marlow, "the philanthropic pretense of the whole concern, . . . their talk, . . . their government, . . . their show of work."

Avowing that he detests lies, Marlow then confesses to misleading the manager's assistant in regard to Marlow's own personal connections. To justify himself, he briefly appeals to the group assembled on the *Nellie* to believe that his concealment was to protect his hopes for Kurtz. At this time, the original narrator mentions how in the dark of the night, Marlow has become no more than a voice, just as Kurtz is no more than a word to Marlow. Also, in order to sustain his own moral composure, Marlow begins to revise reality and tells what could be construed as a lie to his foreman about forthcoming rivets. Instead of rivets, however, the manager's uncle arrives with a band of ivory hunters, calling themselves the Eldorado Exploring Expedition.

Part 2 begins with a conversation between the manager and his uncle to which Marlow is unwillingly privy. The manager's career has been threatened by Kurtz; the manager himself even more so because he does not understand the man who sent them boatloads of ivory and then went back to his station. Marlow concludes that it is because Kurtz is dedicated to his work. Soon afterward, the men forming the expedition leave and are said to have been swallowed up by the wilderness, which Marlow interprets as the insignificance of men in comparison to "the silent wilderness surrounding this cleared speck of earth, waiting patiently for the passing away of this fantastic invasion."

Marlow's steamboat finally repaired, he begins his journey to the Inner Station. He comments that the concentration he devotes to making sure his steamboat does not get sunk causes reality to fade, a peculiar statement that seems a modification of Marlow's previous definition of reality. This alteration in his reality becomes more and more evident as he penetrates "deeper and deeper into the heart of darkness." He fancies that he and his crew are "the first of men taking possession of an accursed inheritance, to be subdued at the cost of profound anguish and of excessive toil." Purveyors of colonialism, like Roman imperialists, are the first men who must face and subdue the wilderness, and Marlow admits that they "are accustomed to look upon the shackled form of a conquered monster, but there—there you could look at a thing monstrous and free." Yet even here, Marlow can look into the face of the men who "howled and leaped, and spun" and find that they too share humanity in common with him. Delving beneath the surface of education and façade, the man who has been made by civilization will encounter the primeval man. The African man who serves as Marlow's fireman is still, solely, a savage at heart, dressed up in civilizing clothes, unconscious of a self separate from the consciousness of the encompassing wilderness. However, although Marlow enters the wilderness and acknowledges this bestial self, he is conscious of another self, his civilized self, which seems to define his "reality."

About 50 miles below the Inner Station, the men come across a hut with some firewood, a note, and a book, *An Inquiry into Some Points of Seamanship*, notated with what Marlow assumes to be cipher. Both he and the manager, superciliously nationalistic, assume the previous visitor to have been English. While they are detained farther downriver on the third morning by a "white fog, . . . as blinding as the night," an anguished, tribal cry resonates in the rain forest. As Marlow surveys the "painfully shocked" expression of his white crew and the "essentially quiet" demeanor and conduct of his black crew while waiting for an attack, he wonders that the greater numbers of cannibals have not preyed on the lesser number of whites and notes the shared trait of restraint in human beings, whether it be the "inborn strength to fight hunger properly" or the manager's desire to "preserve appearances." They are not attacked before the fog lifts, and they continue on. Marlow adopts the impressionistic style of subjective (rather than objective) delineation to describe their approach to what is at first perceived to be an obstructing islet, then a sandbar, and then a series of "shallow patches." Unsuccessfully judging the shoal, Marlow chooses the wrong passage. Consequently, he must steer close to the bank, where they are attacked. In another impressionistic description, the panicked men aboard the steamboat respond to the "little sticks," which turn out to be arrows, by opening fire, shooting into the bushes, reminiscent of the man of war shooting at the unseen "enemy." Howls emerge from the bush, Marlow pulls on the steam whistle, and the frightened attackers retreat. Marlow is struck by the idea that Kurtz is dead and says, disappointedly, that now he will never hear Kurtz speak: "The point was in his being a gifted creature, and that of all his gifts the one that stood out pre-eminently, that carried with it a sense of real presence, was his ability to talk." Marlow seems to have lost interest in substance; what matters is no longer Kurtz's ideas but how he would have expressed himself, the voice having comprised the man. Admitting to the group on the *Nellie* that Kurtz was not dead, however, Marlow launches into a vehement diatribe against the basis of moral failure, the conceit of the individual in society. The insignificance of men compared to the scope and vastness of the wilderness is complemented by their insignificance as individuals in regard to their own society, wherein they function only as negligible toilers in the contest for survival between the greater collectives of society and nature: "your strength comes in . . . your power of devotion, not to yourself, but to an obscure, back-breaking business." Human beings' perceptions of themselves in relation to the world are impairingly subjective. Although Marlow has assumed that his moral self defined the moral world, he now realizes that it has been the constraints of society that have defined his moral reality, not his own self. He says of Kurtz as well: "All Europe contributed to the making of Kurtz." Thus, the International Society for the Suppression of Savage Customs subsequently employs Kurtz to write a report on the superiority of white Europeans, executed eloquently except for an unrestrained postscript written at the bottom: "Exterminate all the brutes!" For the sake of the camaraderie and the bond Marlow felt with his helmsman, a man from the wilderness killed during the attack, Marlow protects the body from further exploitation and tips it unceremoniously over the side of the steamboat. His companions are shocked by this display of heartlessness; the individuals on the expedition who eat human flesh are outraged that a source of food has been forfeited.

Marlow and crew are on the verge of turning back when Marlow spots the Inner Station, where they are cheerfully welcomed by a patchwork-outfitted man who tells them that everything is all right, that the attack was all right (recalling the mustached man at the Central Station and implying that, for all the talk of Kurtz's distinction, the situation is no different here). While the manager and a group of men go on land to fetch Kurtz, Marlow is left with the harlequin, who explains that he is a young Russian adventurer and the one who left them wood and the note at the hut. Marlow returns the book to him and is informed that what he thought was cipher are words in Russian. A very surprised Marlow is struck by the youth's inexplicable existence. "His very existence was improbable," Marlow declares at the beginning of part 3, because he was neither guided by the principles of society (or none that Marlow can understand) nor overcome by the wanton embrace of the wilderness. Lit by the "modest and clear flame" of the "absolutely pure, uncalculating, unpractical spirit of adventure," he has eluded both the darkness of the wilderness and the darkness of civilization. Throughout the novella the passages portraying Africa contain multiple references to intense light, like the "blazing sky" Marlow cites. Light has not metaphorically been what it seems. The darkness the continent contains has been concealed by "blinding sunlight," somewhat like the pale skin of the white men, which has concealed the darkness contained within them.

The knobs of wood on the stakes surrounding Kurtz's house are impressionistically disclosed to be shriveled heads and corroborate Marlow's statement in regard to the necessity of social constraints on a civilized man: "They only showed that Mr. Kurtz lacked restraint in the gratification of his various lusts." As Marlow discovered the deficiency within him, Kurtz, before him, discovered that "the great solitude . . . echoes loudly within him because he was hollow at the core." Although shrouded by a magnificent eloquence, Kurtz, too, is only as ephemeral as his words, a manufactured product of the civilized world. With this revelation, Marlow notices that "the ruined hovel, beyond the symbolic row of stakes" is in the gloom, while he and the steamer "were yet in the sunshine." Kurtz is carried onboard. Onshore, a "wild and gorgeous apparition of a woman," representing the wilderness that had seduced Kurtz, gestures a flamboyant farewell to the boat and "like the wilderness," regards them with "an air of brooding over an inscrutable purpose," recalling the "gloom brooding over a crowd of men." Onboard the steamboat, the manager gleefully decries an unsound Kurtz. As he once turned his back on the station, Marlow turns away from the manager, to Kurtz, and then corrects himself to say that he really had turned to the wilderness; but there, it is no better. He feels "an intolerable weight, . . . the smell of the damp earth, the unseen presence of various corruption." Darkness is everywhere.

Speaking with the harlequin, Marlow advises him to continue as he is, adventuring, assuring the man that "Mr. Kurtz's reputation is safe with me," but uncertain as to how truthful he is being. Marlow is preparing to return to the world of civilization and realizes that appearances must be maintained. During the night, woken by some yelling and drumbeats coming from the forest, he checks on Kurtz in his cabin and receives a shock, "as if something altogether monstrous, intolerable to thought and odious to the soul, had been thrust upon me." Kurtz, whom he has lied for, once the representative for him of civilization's potential, has gone to the wilderness. He does not, however, betray Kurtz, for, "it was ordered I should never betray him—it was written I should be loyal to the nightmare of my choice. I was anxious to deal with this shadow by myself alone." On the bank, he comes upon Kurtz and with restrained desperation says, "You will be lost." Then he unabashedly lies to Kurtz, saying that his reputation has been made and his success in Europe is assured, in order to convince him to return to the boat. Kurtz returns, and they travel back up the river. Finally, the wilderness seems to have bowed its head and to be watching over the steamboat, "this grimy fragment of another world, the forerunner of change, of conquest, of trade, of massacres, of blessings." Marlow watches over Kurtz, for the temptations of the wilderness and of civilization continue to battle him "for the possession of that soul." Marlow witnesses "the inconceivable mystery of a soul that knew no restraint, no faith, and no fear, yet struggling blindly with itself." The boat breaks down, and several nights later, from Kurtz's deathbed, his last words confer the final, despairing assertion that the darkness is truly everywhere, filling everything and everyone: "No eloquence could have been so withering to one's belief in mankind as his final burst of sincerity. 'The horror, the horror.'" Broken in spirit, Marlow succumbs to fever on his return to England. There he is accosted by individuals gripped by their own sense of Kurtz's glorious lineage. Over and over, Marlow lies about Kurtz and suppresses the postscript at the end of the publication for the society in order to maintain the image of the station chief who had once been a man. Marlow's final lie is to Kurtz's fiancée, who asks Marlow what Kurtz's last words had been. Marlow replies that they were her name.

Critical Views

ZDZISŁAW NADJER ON HISTORICAL PERSPECTIVE

He published his most important books between the years 1897
and 1911. It was the time, when on the Continent Maeterlinck
and Strindberg, D'Annunzio and France, Bourget and Chekhov,
and also Andreiev, Björnson, Sudermann, Sienkiewicz and
Hauptmann reached the peak of their fame. Gorki, Thomas
Mann and Gide were just beginning their great careers.
European intellectuals were idolizing Nietzsche and Bergson.
In England Bennett, Galsworthy, Hardy, James, Kipling, Wells
and Wilde were recognized as the leading writers.

With the sole exception of Henry James, another expatriate
and spiritual solitary, there is not another name on this list
which we could link with Conrad's to form a distinct "micro-
group." Therefore it should not be surprising that the early
critics of Conrad had great difficulties in classifying him
and were almost compelled to resort to obviously superficial
formulas, as for example "Kipling of the Malay Archipelago"
or "writer of the sea and adventure." Evidently, he was not an
epigone; but he was not one of the "normal" contemporaries
either. . .

As Jocelyn Baines, Albert J. Guerard and many other critics
have pointed out, Conrad's immediate literary predecessors
were French: he was a diligent disciple of Flaubert and
Maupassant. From Flaubert he took the idea of the novel
as a laboriously shaped work of art; from Maupassant the
impressionistic elements of his literary manifesto in the
famous Preface to The Nigger of the "Narcissus." Also, some
characteristics of his narrative method are best explained by
reference to Flaubert's programme of restrained objective
realism. The writer, advised Flaubert, should be like God:
present everywhere, nowhere visible.

However, we find in Conrad's work elements which cannot
be explained by reference to either his French masters, or his
English contemporaries. For clues, we have to look to Conrad's

biography which reveals that there were in his attitude and background some factors conflicting with Flaubert's model of fiction.

Firstly, and this is perhaps the most important factor of all, the influence of the French realists clashed with the tradition of the Polish Romantics. Secondly, Conrad, a philosophical agnostic, was also sceptical as to the possibilities of a full understanding of the motives of human actions; the monadic separateness of every individual and the inscrutability of forces governing our behaviour formed according to him an obstacle not to be overcome by any amount of intellectual analysis. And thirdly, writing was for him an obviously compensative action: to create meant to make up for the shortcomings, psychological as well as external, of real life. . . .

By the time of Conrad's début the growth of industrial society, the progress of science and the crisis of religious beliefs resulted in a widespread breakdown of established moral codes. Most of contemporary writers were conscious of this process—but nobody more deeply than the desperately probing Dostoevsky, who summed up the age's predicament in a cry, which was supposed to open anew the road to Christianity: "if God does not exist, everything is permissible." Conrad, who hated Dostoevsky and rejected his positive programme, was nevertheless very close to him in the intensity of being aware of the crisis in morality.

The reaction of unrest and alarm was by no means universal in literature. Naturalistic novelists were ready to supplant, without qualms, the newly discovered laws of biology for the old moral dogmas. Popularized Nietzsche and fashionable Wilde were understood as champions of the idea that the rules of the moral game can and should be changed at will: a strong, independent, self-sufficient man's will. And many a writer was inclined to the escapist gesture of turning his back on the whole hideous and nasty world.

Conrad belonged to neither of these groups. He was, like Turgenev and James, conscious that the traditions of enlightened generations were falling apart. Like Flaubert, Maupassant, France and Strindberg, he was shocked by the hypocrisy of the contemporary bourgeois morality. Like Hardy, he was dismayed by the moral plight of man, left defenceless at the mercy of heredity and natural forces. But, unlike Wells, he did not believe in the almost automatically beneficent influence of scientific progress. . . .

Political problems were for Conrad moral problems, fundamentally. "The French Revolution"—he wrote—"was not a political movement at all, but a great outburst of morality."[11] This way of looking at a political conflict as at a massive outburst of moral indignation or depravity was characteristic for many liberal and conservative thinkers. It was, however, usually coupled with a certain degree of either benevolent naiveté, or social ignorance or selfishness. Conrad, unfair as he was to the anarchists, showed an awareness of the existing social conflicts and their sources, and did not have many illusions about the convergence of interests of the haves and the have-nots. For him moral evaluation was not a screen, hiding real social and political issues. . . .

On the larger plane of the general development of fiction, Conrad has bolstered anti-psychologic and anti-naturalistic trends—at a time when naturalism and psychology in the novel ruled supreme. Paradoxically, this avowed individualist and agnostic left a heritage of social and metaphysical concerns. The concentration on types and problems rather than exceptions and psychological subtleties is also a part of his legacy. Whenever we encounter a contemporary novel which deals with moral issues not by way of emphasizing the biological and psychological uniqueness of every person, but by way of looking for the core of [the] common human condition—we may suppose that it runs parallel, or even belongs to the Conrad tradition.

Concentrating on general problems and typical situations is in Conrad's work one of the means to overcome the oppressive consciousness of man's loneliness. He was intensely aware of the all-pervading problem of uprootedness and isolation; more so than any of his contemporaries or any writer since, with the possible exception of Kafka. "We live, as we dream—alone." Solitude was for Conrad an element of the human condition that is inescapable—but against which we should fight relentlessly (here he differed from the fatalistic Kafka). In view of our present preoccupation with alienation and with the individual's loneliness within mass society and in the face of a universe expanding in all directions—Conrad seems to be a prophet. But not a despairing prophet of helplessness in the face of unavoidable doom.

Note
11. *A Personal Record* (Dent Collected Ed.), p. 95.

PETER EDGERLY FIRCHOW ON ENVISIONING KURTZ

In the "Author's Note" that he wrote in 1917 on the occasion of the republication of *Youth* in the edition of his collected works, Conrad remarks of *Heart of Darkness* that, like "Youth," it is a story based on "experience too; but it is experience pushed a little (and only very little) beyond the actual facts of the case for the perfectly legitimate, I believe, purpose of bringing it home to the minds and bosoms of the readers" (*HD* 4). In the years since Conrad wrote these words, a great deal of effort has been expended by critics and biographers in attempting to gauge the precise nature and degree of actual personal "experience" in the story. (If the spirit of Conrad is somewhere gazing down on these efforts, I think he too must be impressed by their awful extent and efficiency.) According to Norman Sherry, who has led the way here, Conrad was not being quite ingenuous when he claimed to have "pushed" his own experience only a "very little" beyond the "actual facts." After having dug long and deep in contemporaneous publications and records (including those of the Belgian Company, which originally employed Conrad), Sherry has been able to point out numerous significant deviations both from Conrad's own biographical experience and from the larger historical context[1] (*Western* 9–136). . . .

Taking note of all of these alterations to his own experience in *Heart of Darkness* is important in allowing us to ascertain more exactly what it was that Conrad meant to bring home, as his 1917 "Author's Note" put it, "to the minds and bosoms of the readers." This is especially the case with one highly significant change not yet mentioned, namely the addition of a character who appears to have had an only minimal basis in the reality of Conrad's African experience. This, of course, is Kurtz. Although it has long been known that the *Roi des Belges* picked up at Stanley Falls a gravely ill company agent named Georges Antoine Klein, who was a French national and who died on the voyage back; and although it has also been known that in the manuscript version, the first few references to Kurtz were originally to Klein, there is no evidence that, beyond the purely external circumstances of his death and his analogous German name (Klein means "small" in German), Klein's life or character bore any meaningful resemblance to the life and character ascribed by Marlow to Kurtz.[6] Norman Sherry devotes a whole chapter of his book to demonstrating why the innocuous Klein has (perhaps fortunately for him) no claim to be mistaken for Kurtz. Sherry devotes another chapter to proving that, instead, "at least in part the inspiration for Kurtz" was Klein's immediate superior, the highly enterprising Belgian military officer Arthur Hodister. According to Sherry, Hodister was well known as a man of considerable ability and integrity; he was responsible for some intrepid exploring, collected a large quantity of ivory, did some writing for newspapers in Belgium, and had influential friends in Europe. Though Conrad probably never met Hodister personally, Sherry is convinced that he must have heard of him from various sources, much as Marlow hears of Kurtz in the story.

Sherry's identification of Hodister is highly speculative, not only in terms of what Conrad "must" have known about him (and how), but with regard to Hodister himself. Among other things, Sherry hypothesizes a possible rivalry between Hodister and Alexandre Delcommune (the original model for the Manager's uncle), as well as a dislike for him on the part of the latter's brother, Camille Delcommune (the Manager himself). So far as any actual evidence is concerned, all of these speculations are without foundation.[7] Most damaging of all, Sherry fails to acknowledge fully the radical differences between the ways in which Hodister and Kurtz met their deaths, and therefore he fails to take into account the profoundly differing implications of those deaths. In the case of Hodister, he died, according to the report from the London *Times* reprinted by Sherry, at the hands of treacherous Arab slave traders while attempting to negotiate an armistice. Upon the failure of the negotiations, Hodister and his two white companions were taken prisoner, tortured, and decapitated. Their heads were stuck on poles and their bodies were eaten. Of all this Sherry observes, with remarkable understatement, that "Hodister's fate was not precisely that of Kurtz." He then goes on to confuse the issue further by proposing grandly that "it might be said of both men that their faith in their ability to command the 'exotic immensity' of the Congo jungle led to their being destroyed by that same Immensity—by its inhabitants in the case of Hodister and its primitive customs in the case of Kurtz" (*Western* 110–11).

Just what Sherry means by Kurtz's having been destroyed by "primitive customs" is puzzling, since one of the few points of similarity between Kurtz and Klein is the fact that both unmistakably died of tropical fever (probably malaria), the most common cause of death among whites in nineteenth-century Central Africa. Ironically, Kurtz is a man of violence who dies (though not peacefully) in bed. Hodister, on the other hand—at least if one is to believe contemporaneous news reports, which is all we, or Sherry for that matter, have to go on—was a military man who met a violent death while trying to make peace. If, therefore, Conrad did indeed take him even "in part" as a model for Kurtz, it could only have been in order to denigrate the activities of the agents of Leopold II by a nasty species of character assassination. If so, this would fall squarely under the rubric of what Batchelor sees as Conrad's plan to show how all Europeans (with the notable exception of Marlow) are propagators of "mindless cruelty." It is, I confess, an explanation that strikes me not only as unlikely in itself but also as utterly uncharacteristic of Conrad's generally responsible use of biographical and historical material. This is not an explanation, I should hasten to add, proposed by Sherry himself, who, in the final analysis, provides no explanation at all as to why Conrad might have chosen so unlikely a model as Hodister for Kurtz.[8]

It may not be surprising, therefore, that Hodister has not been widely accepted as "the" original for Kurtz. Of recent biographers only Roger Tennant (80) and Jeffrey Meyers (*Conrad* 104) follow Sherry's lead here. But if not Hodister, then who? The answer unfortunately is—multitudes. Starting off, as Sherry does, with Klein and Hodister, Ian Watt adds a series of further possibilities, most of them already suggested by earlier critics: Emin Pasha (born Eduard Schnitzer in Germany), whom Stanley attempted to relieve in 1887 and who was killed by Arabs in 1892; the Englishman Edmund Barttelot, in charge of Stanley's rear guard during the Emin Pasha Relief Expedition and killed in a skirmish (favored by Jerry Allen); Charles Henry Stokes, an Irish ivory trader summarily hanged by a Belgian officer, Lothaire, in 1895; Carl Peters, the notoriously cruel German explorer of East Africa (proposed by Hannah Arendt); the French captain Paul Voulet, who imitated Peters's example in Senegal; and last but certainly not least, the infamous/famous Anglo-American explorer who more than any other single figure helped establish the Western stereotype of "darkest Africa" (a stereotype echoed by Conrad's title)[9] and who served as Leopold II's principal agent in the early stages of Congo exploration and exploitation, Henry Morgan Stanley. Of Stanley, Watt remarks that he is "probably of central importance, though not so much as a basis for the character of Kurtz as for the moral atmosphere in which he was created" (*Conrad* 142:45).[10]

None of these models quite fits Kurtz, some because they were, so far as we know, simply taking part in officially sponsored military-commercial expeditions or else too "selfless" in their devotion to the cause of antislavery (Hodister as well as Barttelot and the others); or because they were more victims of Arab atrocities than perpetrators of individual acts of aggression themselves (Hodiste Barttelot, and the others again); or because they were too private and obscure in their work (Klein and Stokes); or, finally, because they were too prominent and successful (Emin Pasha, Peters, and especially Stanley). None of them appears to have committed anything like the brutal "raiding" of villages, using warrior tribes as the means, that Kurtz does in *Heart of Darkness*. This is a "system" that in fact was notoriously a specialty of the Arabs, notably of Tippo Tib, whose headquarters were at Stanley Falls (the Inner Station).[11] From all this it seems most reasonable or, at any rate, least problematic to conclude, as Najder does, that "the model for Kurtz was supplied on the one hand by literary and philosophical tradition, on the other by the behavior of a great many Europeans in Africa. In the end as a character with his own specific life history, Kurtz is the author's own creation" (*Joseph Conrad* 526).

That Conrad meant Kurtz to be thought of more as a representative or, as he remarked himself, a *symbolic* character rather than as the fictional rendering of a particular individual also seems evident from the general way in which Kurtz conforms to the description of company officials in the Congo provided by Robert Brown in 1895. After suggesting that those officials who were stationed on the lower reaches of the Congo were, generally speaking, law-abiding, he adds that in the case of those "working" along the upper reaches (the location of Kurtz's Inner Station), "where the natives are more savage, and infinitely more difficult to deal with, martial law is entrusted to young officials, poorly paid, often of slender ability, not always of the best character, and invariably beyond the checks afforded by the presence of those whose example authority might restrain the exercise of petty despotism. The natives have been treated as if they were slaves, and otherwise irritate in a manner little calculated to endear the white man and the white man's ways" (183). Kurtz, in other words, should probably be thought of as a deliberately fictional character who shares traits with a wide variety of Europeans who worked or traveled in the vicinity of Stanley Falls in the 1880s and 1890s rather than as the embodiment of a specifically identifiable historical personage.

Notes

1. The first systematic attempt to correlate Conrad's personal experience of the Congo with the account provided in *Heart of Darkness* is Gérard Jean-Aubry's *Joseph Conrad in the Congo* (1926), which makes extensive use of Conrad's "Congo Diary" and his correspondence, as well as contemporaneous Belgian publications. Though Jean-Aubry occasionally takes note of evident differences, such as the absence of any model for the Chief Accountant, he does not ascribe these to any deliberate desire on Conrad's part to effect changes. Instead, they apparently derive, implicitly or explicitly, from inadequate biographical knowledge on our part. So Jean-Aubry is sure Kurtz must have been modeled on someone Conrad knew personally. In his view, this person was Georges Antoine Klein, who died aboard the *Roi des Belges* as it steamed back downriver from Stanley Falls under Conrad's temporary command (*Congo* 65 66). Jean-Aubry develops this hypothesis more fully in his biography of Conrad, where, even though unable to cite any specific evidence, he affirms his conviction that there is between Klein and Kurtz "much more in common than a mere similarity in names." Of this he says, "there can be no doubt in the mind of anybody who knows Conrad's psychological method" (*Life* 136). Unlike subsequent biographical critics such as Sherry, Jean-Aubry pretty much takes Conrad's claims regarding the close biographical basis of his story literally.

6. In the view at least of the Belgians, Klein's status was so insignificant that he was not provided with an entry in the exhaustive biographical lexicon of Belgian colonial activity, the *Biographie Coloniale Belge*. The *BCB* does, however, have an entry for a Danish national named Hans-Lindholm Kurtzhals, a sometime lieutenant in the Royal Danish Navy, who in June 1892 captained the *Ville de Gand* on its way to Stanley Falls with the notorious Lothaire aboard. After participating in the Arab wars, Kurtzhals completed his service in the Congo in 1900 as captain of the Port of Banana (*BCB* 5:516–17). Why Conrad chose to change the name from Klein to Kurtz is not clear. Ian Watt is apparently indulging his fancy when he remarks that in changing the name from Klein to Kurtz, Conrad was evoking "a much more sonorous and menacing sound" (*Conrad* 137).

7. There is, of course, no doubt that Conrad himself felt a hearty dislike for the two Delcommune brothers and would no doubt have been pleased to find further evidence of their skullduggery. Given the fact, however, that Hodister's position vis-à-vis Alexandre Delcommune was far more secure than that of Kurtz vis-à-vis the Manager, it seems unlikely that he would have been quite so easily outmaneuvered as Kurtz supposedly is. That whites often quarreled among themselves is, of course, something Conrad was fully aware of. Indeed, his other story about Africa, "An Outpost of Progress,"

is based on that perception. Some thirty years later Evelyn Waugh's description (174–75) of an absurd misunderstanding between himself and the captain of a Congo paddle-steamer may owe something to Conrad's depiction of the comic aspects of such quarrels.

8. As Jean Stengers points out, the idea that Conrad may have had Hodister in mind when creating Kurtz was suggested as long ago as 1929 by Léon Guébels. Even so, Stengers finds the identification with Hodister unpersuasive, explicitly agreeing here with the 1971 *TLS* review of Sherry's book ("Leopold's" 752–54, 760). In *Conrad and His World* (1972), however, Sherry makes no mention of Hodister but refers only to Klein as "the model for Kurtz" (62).

9. Achebe is not alone in finding Conrad's association of Africa with "darkness" at least potentially offensive (*HD* 261). Even a defender of Conrad's story such as Frances Singh wonders if Marlow does not push the metaphoric implications of the title too far in a racist direction (271). More generally, Benita Parry writes of the title that it "registers its manifold preoccupations . . . by signifying a geographical location, a metaphysical landscape and a theological category," thereby addressing itself "simultaneously to Europe's exploitation of Africa, the primeval human situation, an archaic aspect of the mind's structure and a condition of moral baseness" (20). Conrad himself may have felt some qualms about the title, for in "Geography and some Explorers" he goes out of his way to say that the atlas that he used as a boy, dating from 1852, "knew nothing, of course, of the Great Lakes. The heart of its African [*sic*] was white and big." A few pages later he tells of being derided by his schoolmates when he put his finger "on a spot in the middle of the then white heart of Africa" (*Last Essays* 20, 24). The equivalent passages in *Heart of Darkness* and *A Personal Record* refer instead to "blank spaces" and make no mention of any "heart." In *Journey without Maps* Graham Greene makes a novel association between "heart" and the map of Africa. He thinks of Africa not as a "particular place, but a shape, a strangeness, a wanting to know . . . the shape, of course, is roughly that of the human heart" (17). Some critics, however, have reacted negatively to Conrad's supposed "blanking" out of Africa. Thus, Christopher Miller notes the "absence" of Africa as a *name* in the story, along with all other African place names (except for quasi-humorous ones like Gran' Bassam and Little Popo). He does not, however, mention the equally absent Belgium or Brussels or, for that matter, the absent London (175). Terry Eagleton, too, hears "at the centre of each of Conrad's works . . . a resonant silence," though it is not specifically a silence associated with the suppression of place names (137). According to Cedric Watts, the absent names have an altogether different significance; they represent Conrad's subtle device for drawing the British reader into an awareness of his complicity with the imperialist

abuses in the heart of darkness: "by never actually calling the company Belgian or the region the Congo" and by stressing Kurtz's English and cosmopolitan origins, he "makes it impossible for the British reader to stand smugly aloof from the indictment of imperialism." Suggestive as this argument is, it would follow from the same reasoning that, since the Belgians are also *not* named, their (or their king's) empire is not being specifically impugned (*Preface* 127). Andrea White, however, reaches a conclusion similar to Watts's solely on the basis of Kurtz's partially British origins ("Conrad" 192).

10. Aside from the by now familiar assertion that Kurtz is Marlow's (and perhaps also Conrad's) "double" (Burden, *Heart* 101), various attempts have been made to link Kurtz more or less closely with Conrad's own father (Batchelor 84), with Nietzsche and Schopenhauer (Burden, *Heart* 43), with David Livingstone (Jean-Aubry, *Life* 2:121), and with Cecil Rhodes (Hay 113). Jane Ford proposes Roger Casement as a possible model, citing a 1923 New York interview with Conrad (129). Molly Mahood suggests J.S. Jameson, another member of Stanley's Emin Pasha relief expedition, as a possibility; she also points to Pierre Mille's story "Le Vieux du Zambèse" as providing a literary parallel (25–26). Yves Hervouet also mentions Rimbaud's *Une Saison en enfer* and Loti's *Le Roman d'un spahi*, as well as echoes of Flaubert and Maupassant (63). Peter Knox-Shaw tries to make a case for identifying Kurtz with the explorer Richard Burton on the basis of the latter's admitted participation in "the dance that initiated the complex rituals of human sacrifice," as well as his great intellect and diabolical reputation (147–48). To this already ample and very mixed bag one might add the name of the Belgian captain Guillaume Van Kerckhoven, who belonged to what might be called the antislavery "gang of virtue" and who apparently was killed accidentally in August 1892 while leading an exploratory mission from the Congo to the Nile. Van Kerckhoven's mother's surname was Miller, possibly indicating English ancestry. In 1891 he became notorious for confiscating ivory worth hundreds of thousands of francs from Arab caravans on the pretext of freeing their slaves. In the process he and his forces killed an estimated eighteen hundred men. In this way Van Kerckhoven helped provoke the outbreak of the so-called Arab Wars, which lasted until 1894 (Ceulemans 326–31). Conrad may have crossed paths with Van Kerckhoven on the latter's arrival in Boma at the beginning of December 1890. According to Albert Chapaux, an early historian of the Congo Free State, Van Kerckhoven deserved to be placed in the first rank of those who contributed to the development of the colony (*BCB* 1:565–73; Bourne 147–64). Jules Marchal also links Kurtz with Van Kerckhoven in his brief discussion of *Heart of Darkness* (Marchal, 1:169). Worth considering too is the possibility that

Conrad may have meant his readers to think of Leopold II himself as a kind of ultimate model for Kurtz. In terms of physique (bald, very tall) Leopold certainly resembled Kurtz, as he did also in personality. Leopold was an immensely energetic and egotistical man, given to vastly ambitious plans and partly deceived by his own hypocrisy but at the same time also motivated by a curious kind of altruism. Like Kurtz, too, "all Europe contributed to the making of Leopold (*HD* 50). His Cousin Victoria was Queen of England (Kurtz's mother is half-English) and his knowledge of English was nearly as good as his French. Like Kurtz again, Leopold had a German surname (Saxe-Coburg), though his mother was the daughter of the last French king, Louis Phillippe. Also, if we think of the characters of the Amazon and the Intended in allegorical terms as representing, respectively, the Congo and Belgium, Leopold, like Kurtz, has deceived and betrayed—and profoundly touched the lives of—both. Like Kurtz, he was undoubtedly a "remarkable man."

11. This "system" is described in detail by Captain Guillaume Van Kerckhoven in Salmon (*Le Voyage* 76). In his report to the governor-general of the Congo Free State, Van Kerckhoven describes how Arabs habitually attack villages without warning; kill everyone who offers resistance, including women; take the remaining women and children prisoner; and then pillage and lay waste to the buildings. Several days later, they enter into negotiations with the returning male villagers, exchanging prisoners for ivory and leaving behind a garrison to ensure further deliveries. The actual raiders were not Arabs themselves but mostly members of previously subjugated tribes who were provided with guns and ammunition for the purpose of carrying out these raids under Arab leadership. (See also the Appendix or a more impartial description of this "system" of trade.) As none other than H.M. Stanley himself pointed out, however, this was a "system" (sans the essential ivory component to be sure) that the Arabs did not invent. It was, in Stanley's view, a system devised and perfected by the British themselves in the seventeenth century: "[T]he system adopted by the British crews in those days was very similar to that employed by the Arabs to-day in inner Africa. They landed at night, surrounded the affected village, and then set fire to the huts, and as the frightened people issued out of the burning houses, they were seized and carried to the ships; or sometimes the skipper, in his hurry for sea, sent his crew to range through the town he was trading with, and, regardless of rank, to seize upon every man, woman, and child they met" ("Slavery" 614). Later in the same essay Stanley describes, in terms similar to those used by Van Kerckhoven, the methods practiced by Tippo Tib and other Arabs to obtain ivory.

Albert J. Guerard on Marlow as Central Character

The autobiographical basis of the narrative is well known, and its introspective bias obvious; this is Conrad's longest journey into self. But it is well to remember that "Heart of Darkness" is also other if more superficial things: a sensitive and vivid travelogue, and a comment on "the vilest scramble for loot that ever disfigured the history of human conscience and geographical exploration."[1] The Congo was much in the public mind in 1889, when Henry Stanley's relief expedition found Emin Pasha (who like Kurtz did not want to be rescued), and it is interesting to note that Conrad was in Brussels during or immediately after Stanley's triumphant welcome there in April 1890. This was just before he set out on his own Congo journey. We do not know how much the Georges Antoine Klein who died on board the *Roi des Belges* resembled the fictional Kurtz, but Stanley himself provided no mean example of a man who could gloss over the extermination of savages with pious moralisms which were very possibly "sincere."

"Heart of Darkness" thus has its important public side, as an angry document on absurd and brutal exploitation. . . .

In any event it is time to recognize that the story is not primarily about Kurtz or about the brutality of Belgian officials but about Marlow its narrator. To what extent it also expresses the Joseph Conrad a biographer might conceivably recover, who in 1898 still felt a debt must be paid for his Congo journey and who paid it by the writing of this story, is doubtless an insoluble question. . . .

Substantially and in its central emphasis "Heart of Darkness" concerns Marlow (projection to whatever great or small degree of a more irrecoverable Conrad) and his journey toward and through certain facets or potentialities of self. F.R. Leavis seems to regard him as a narrator only, providing a "specific and concretely realized point of view."[5] But Marlow reiterates often enough that he is recounting a spiritual voyage of self-discovery. He remarks casually but crucially that he did not know himself before setting out, and that he likes work for the chance it provides to "find yourself . . . what no other man can ever know." The Inner Station "was the farthest point of navigation and the culminating point of my experience." At a material and rather superficial level, the journey is through the temptation of atavism.[6] It is a record of "remote kinship" with the "wild and passionate uproar," of a "trace of a response" to it, of a final rejection of the "fascination of the abomination." And why should there not be the trace of a response? "The mind of man is capable of anything—because everything is in it, all the past as well as all the future." Marlow's temptation is made concrete through his exposure to Kurtz, a white man and sometime idealist who had fully responded to the wilderness: a potential and fallen self. "I had turned to the wilderness really, not to Mr. Kurtz." At the climax Marlow follows Kurtz ashore, confounds the beat of the drum with the beating of his heart, goes through the ordeal of looking into Kurtz's "mad soul," and brings him back to the ship. He returns to Europe a changed and more knowing man. Ordinary people are now "intruders whose knowledge of life was to me an irritating pretence, because I felt so sure they could not possibly know the things I knew."

On this literal plane, and when the events are so abstracted from the dream-sensation conveying them, it is hard to take Marlow's plight very seriously. Will he, the busy captain and moralizing narrator, also revert to savagery, go ashore for a howl and a dance, indulge unspeakable lusts? The late Victorian reader (and possibly Conrad himself) could take this more seriously than we; could literally believe not merely in a Kurtz's deterioration through months of solitude but also in the sudden reversions to the "beast" of naturalistic fiction. Insofar as Conrad does want us to take it seriously and literally, we must admit the nominal triumph of a currently accepted but false psychology over his own truer intuitions. But the triumph is only nominal. For the personal narrative is unmistakably authentic, which means that it explores something truer, more fundamental, and distinctly less material: the night journey into the unconscious, and confrontation of an entity within the self.

"I flung one shoe overboard, and became aware that that was exactly what I had been looking forward to—a talk with Kurtz." It little matters what, in terms of psychological symbolism, we call this double or say he represents: whether the Freudian id or the Jungian shadow or more vaguely the outlaw. And I am afraid it is impossible to say where Conrad's conscious understanding of his story began and ended. The important thing is that the introspective plunge and powerful dream seem true; and are therefore inevitably moving. . . .

The travelogue as travelogue is not to be ignored; and one of Roger Casement's consular successors in the Congo (to whom I introduced "Heart of Darkness" in 1957) remarked at once that Conrad certainly had a "feel for the country." The demoralization of the first company station is rendered by a boiler "wallowing in the grass," by a railway truck with its wheels in the air. Presently Marlow will discover a scar in the hillside into which drainage pipes for the settlement had been tumbled: then will walk into the grove where the Negroes are free to die in a "greenish gloom." The sharply visualized particulars suddenly intrude on the somber intellectual flow of Marlow's meditation: magnified, arresting. The boilermaker who "had to crawl in the mud under the bottom of the steamboat . . . would tie up that beard of his in a kind of white serviette he brought for the purpose. It had loops to go over his ears." The papier-mâché Mephistopheles is as vivid, with his delicate hooked nose and glittering mica eyes. So too is Kurtz's harlequin companion and admirer humbly dissociating himself from the master's lusts and gratifications. "I! I! I am a simple man. I have no great thoughts." And even Kurtz, shadow and symbol though he be, the man of eloquence who in this story is almost voiceless, and necessarily so— even Kurtz is sharply visualized, an "animated image of death," a skull and body emerging as from a winding sheet, "the cage of his ribs all astir, the bones of his arm waving."

This is Africa and its flabby inhabitants; Conrad did indeed have a "feel for the country." Yet the dark tonalities and final brooding impression derive as much from rhythm and rhetoric as from such visual details: derive from the high aloof ironies and from a prose that itself advances and recedes in waves. "This initiated wraith from the back of Nowhere honored me with its amazing confidence before it vanished altogether." Or, "It is strange how I accepted this unforeseen partnership, this choice of nightmares forced upon me in the tenebrous land invaded by these mean and greedy phantoms." These are true Conradian rhythms, but they are also rhythms of thought. The immediate present can be rendered with great compactness and drama: the ship staggering within ten feet of the bank at the time of the attack, and Marlow's sudden glimpse of a face amongst the leaves, then of the bush "swarming with human limbs." But still more immediate and personal, it may be, are the meditative passages evoking vast tracts of time, and the "first of men taking possession of an accursed inheritance." The prose is varied far more so than is usual in the early work, both in rhythm and in the movements from the general to the particular and back. But the shaped sentence collecting and fully expending its breath appears to be the norm. Some of the best passages begin and end with them:

"Going up that river was like traveling back to the earliest beginnings of the world, when vegetation rioted on the earth and the big trees were kings. An empty stream, a great silence, an impenetrable forest. The air was warm, thick, heavy, sluggish. There was no joy in the brilliance of sunshine. The long stretches of the waterway ran on, deserted, into the gloom of overshadowed distances. On silvery sandbanks hippos and alligators sunned themselves side by side."

The insistence on darkness, finally, and quite apart from ethical or mythical overtone, seems a right one for this extremely personal statement. There is a darkness of passivity, paralysis, immobilization: it is from the state of entranced languor rather than from the monstrous desires that the double Kurtz, this shadow, must be saved. In Freudian theory, we are told, such preoccupation may indicate fear of the feminine and passive. But may it not also be connected, through one of the spirit's multiple disguises, with a radical fear of death, that other darkness? "I had turned to the wilderness really, not to Mr. Kurtz, who, I was ready to admit, was as good as buried. And for a moment it seemed to me as if I also were buried in a vast grave full of unspeakable secrets. I felt an intolerable weight oppressing my breast, the smell of the damp earth, the unseen presence of victorious corruption, the darkness of an impenetrable night."

It would be folly to try to limit the menace of vegetation in the restless life of Conradian image and symbol. But the passage reminds us again of the story's reflective references, and its images of deathly immobilization in grass. Most striking are the black shadows dying in the greenish gloom of the grove at the first station. But grass sprouts between the stones of the European city, a "whited sepulcher," and on the same page Marlow anticipates coming upon the remains of his predecessor: "the grass growing through his ribs was tall enough to hide his bones." The critical meeting with Kurtz occurs on a trail through the grass. Is there not perhaps an intense horror behind the casualness with which Marlow reports his discoveries, say of the Negro with the bullet in his forehead? Or: "Now and then a carrier dead in harness, at rest in the long grass near the path, with an empty water gourd and his lone staff lying by his side."

All this, one must acknowledge, does not make up an ordinary light travelogue.

Notes

1. *Last Essays*, p. 17. [See "Geography and Some Explorers" in this Norton Critical Edition.] In "Heart of Darkness" Conrad makes once his usual distinction between British imperialism and the imperialism of other nations. On the map in Brussels there "was a vast amount of red— good to see at any time, because one knows that some real work is done in there." His 1899 letters to E. L. Sanderson and to Mme. Angèle Zagórska on the Boer war express his position clearly. The conspiracy to oust the Briton "is read to be hatched in other regions. It . . . is everlastingly skulking in the Far East. A war there or anywhere but in S. Africa would have been conclusive,—would have been worth the sacrifices" (Jean-Aubry, *Life and Letters*, I. 286). "That they—the Boers—are struggling in good faith for their independence

cannot be doubted: but it is also a fact that they have no idea of liberty, which can only be found under the English flag all over the world" (*Ibid.*, I, 288).

2. F. R. Leavis. *The Great Tradition* (London, 1948), p. 183.

6. Regression to a primitive state. [Editor]

JAKOB LOTHE ON CONRADIAN NARRATIVE

Conradian narrative requires not only close reading, but frequently re-reading as well. To focus on textual structure does not, however, imply that a literary text exists in a historical and cultural vacuum; nor does it follow that the connections between the historical author and the text's various narrative constituents are unimportant. In a sense, the opposition between locutions such as 'narrative', on the one hand, and 'history', on the other, is factitious, possibly even theoretically untenable: 'it is only on the level of structures that we can describe literary development' (Todorov, *Introduction to Poetics*, p. 61). Any discussion of Conrad's fictional achievement needs then to include some consideration of its narrative form.

Writing of 'Heart of Darkness', Peter Madsen notes that

> Language is more than a dictionary and a grammar, but this 'more' is not, as the formalist-structuralist poetics would have it, like a specifically literary grammar which is neutral in relation to experience. Literary forms are formulations of experience—they are, as Adorno puts it, sedimentation of experience . . . The narrative forms are of this kind. Any new story is related to earlier stories to the extent that these have interfered with the author's formulation of experience . . . But the word 'narrative' is ambiguous. Pointing beyond the text itself, it refers not only to the chain of events (the 'story'), but also to the act of narration. ('Modernity and melancholy', p. 100)

This is a nuanced view of the complicated relationship between personal experience and literary text. The observation

46

can, for instance, be related to the numerous intertextual echoes in 'Heart of Darkness'—from Virgil via Dante to more recent travel literature. It can also be related to Conrad's use of Marlow as the main narrator.

The introduction of Marlow marks a turning-point in Conradian narrative. This shift is not merely technical, but intimately connected with Conrad's uncertainty and experimentation as a writer of fiction. Zdzislaw Najder helpfully comments on Marlow's importance for Conrad's writing:

> Marlow, a model English gentleman, ex-officer of the merchant marine, was the embodiment of all that Conrad would wish to be if he were to become completely anglicized. And since that was not the case, and since he did not quite share his hero's point of view, there was no need to identify himself with Marlow, either emotionally or intellectually. Thanks to Marlow's duality, Conrad could feel solidarity with, and a sense of belonging to, England by proxy, at the same time maintaining a distance such as one has toward a creation of one's imagination. Thus, Conrad, although he did not permanently resolve his search for a consistent consciousness of self-identity, found an integrating point of view that enabled him, at last, to break out of the worst crisis of his writing career. (*Joseph Conrad: A Chronicle*, p. 231)

This comment is persuasive partly because of its implied suggestion that, for Conrad, Marlow is not only a main narrator and an important character, but a distancing device that helps the author control and shape his fictional material. In a classic essay published as early as 1912, Edward Bullough regarded 'distance' as the quality that gives an expression aesthetic validity: 'Distancing means the separation of personal affections, whether idea or complex experience, from the concrete personality of the experience' ('Psychical distance', p. 127). Thus understood, the concept serves to identify one of the most distinctive aspects of Conradian narrative. As far as Conrad is concerned, Bullough's general observation blends into the author's *need for distance* both from his fiction and, in a complex way, from his audience, in order to write at all. The concept of distance needs, however, to be diversified to be helpful critically. The most important variants are temporal, spatial, and attitudinal distance. In 'Heart of Darkness', there is a significant temporal distance between Conrad's personal experience in the Congo in 1890, on which the fiction is based, and the time of the novella's writing approximately eight years later. There is also a very considerable spatial distance between London, the setting of the narrative act, and the Congo, the place of the main action. Finally, the temporal and spatial distances are related to the 'attitudinal' distance, the ideological perspectives of the narrator(s) and the implied author. This last variant is the most complex because it is more closely connected with the varying levels of insight of the implied author, the narrator, and character, and because it is, as a critical metaphor, related to the reader's interpretive activity.

A good illustration of modulations of distance is provided by the opening of 'Heart of Darkness'. The novella begins by introducing us to a narrative setting that establishes a peculiarly static frame around the main action. A group of five men are aboard a cruising yawl, waiting for the turn of the tide:

> The sea-reach of the Thames stretched before us like the beginning of an interminable waterway. In the offing the sea and the sky were welded together without a joint, and in the luminous space the tanned sails of the barges drifting up with the tide seemed to stand still in red clusters of canvas sharply peaked, with gleams of varnished sprits. (p. 135)

The visual qualities of this introductory description resemble those often referred to in discussions of Conrad's literary impressionism. Suggesting a first-person narrative, the pronoun 'us' refers to the five characters aboard the *Nellie*. One of them is Marlow; however, not Marlow but an anonymous first-person narrator is speaking here. This frame narrator introduces us to the setting of the novella as well as to Marlow as the main narrator. When Marlow is duly introduced and embarks on his tale, the function of the frame narrator becomes more complex, since he also becomes a *narratee* in the group Marlow addresses.[6] To put this another way: in accordance with the narrative convention employed, the frame narrator functions first as a narratee, and then as a first-person narrator relaying Marlow's story to the reader. The phrase 'narrative convention' is necessary because the time of traditional, simple narratives is over in 'Heart of Darkness'. At first sight, the novella's narrative situation seems to resemble what Wolfgang's Kayser calls *epische Ursituation* (*Das sprachliche Kunstwerke*, p. 349), that is, the 'original' narrative situation in which a narrator is telling his audience something that has happened. (If related to the historical metanarrative, this is the narrative situation of *Gemeinschaft*.) However interesting, the resemblance is none the less superficial—not only because Kayser's concept of original narrative situation excludes the device of the frame narrator, but also because in 'Heart of Darkness' both the narrative act and its motivations are much more problematic.

In the classic frame narrative the frame narrator is often the most authoritative and knowledgeable of the narrators. This is not so in 'Heart of Darkness'. For although the frame narrator passes on Marlow's story and appears to be reliable, his insights are distinctly inferior to Marlow's. A second example will illustrate this point. Having finished his introductory description, the narrator exclaims: 'What greatness had not floated on the ebb of that river into the mystery of an unknown earth! ... The dreams of men, the seed of commonwealths, the germs of empires' (p. 137). Isolated from its context, the exclamation sounds like a piece of imperialistic rhetoric. This impression increases the impact and suggestiveness of Marlow's first words: 'And this also ... has been one of the dark places of the earth' (p. 138).

This narrative variation is one of the most effective in all of Conrad's fiction. Marlow's remark exposes the relative naïveté and limited insight of the frame narrator and prefigures the complex, sombre implications of the tale he is about to tell. . . . . The use of a narrator is a distancing device, and 'Heart of Darkness' accentuates the distancing process by the use of two narrators rather than one. At the same time, the novella is also a good example of a text where distancing narrative devices paradoxically increase the reader's attention and interest. Conrad effectively exploits the conventional or common character of the frame narrator to make Marlow's story more plausible. The frame narrative manipulates the reader into a position resembling that of the frame narrator *as narratee*, a position distinguished by a meditative but broadly accepting response to the disillusioned insights of Marlow's story. This effect is particularly evident in the novella's last paragraph, which is spoken by the frame narrator. Echoing the numerous references to 'darkness', its concluding words—'immense darkness' (p. 252)—repeat Marlow's last words in the paragraph above. . . .

Rather than attempt to summarize the author's various narrative techniques, it is more helpful to conclude by stressing three of its key characteristics.

First, although Conradian narrative may usefully be grouped into third- and first-person narratives, several of his most important texts contain elements of both. These two main variants of Conradian narrative are remarkably flexible. . . .

Secondly, Conrad's fictional work is distinguished by a tendency towards paradox, one of which is that: 'A declared fear of the corrosive and faith-destroying intellect—[is] doubled by a profound and ironic skepticism' (Guerard, *Conrad the Novelist*, p. 57). Although such paradoxes identify tensions in the literary *content* of Conrad's fiction, these tensions or conflicts are shaped, dramatized, and intensified through his narrative. In 'Heart of Darkness' and *Lord Jim*, for example, the pressure towards paradox is inseparable from Conrad's oblique narrative method—including the complicated, unstable relations between the different narrators and characters. 'Conrad's tragic awareness of the reciprocal but conflicting demands of the individual and of society' (Watt, *Conrad in the*

50

Nineteenth Century, pp. 358–9) is also in a sense paradoxical; and it suggests interesting affinities with, as well as significant differences from, major Modernist writers such as Hamsun, Proust, Kafka, and Joyce.

This observation blends into a concluding comment. For Conrad, narrative experimentation is not an aim in itself, but strengthens the dialectical relationship between narrative technique and thematics in his work. Thus we have seen, for example, that Jim is 'under a cloud' (*LJ*, p. 416) because his problem is *intrinsically* difficult: therefore it is convincing that neither Marlow as narrator nor we as readers can see him clearly. The relationship between Conrad and his narrators is complicated, but it surely does not follow that it is unimportant. In Conrad's fiction, the narrator's relationship with the story told cannot be separated from the author's relationship with his work—and, by implication, with the world that the work portrays.

Note

6. The narratee is the agent who is at least implicitly, and in Conrad often also explicitly, addressed by the narrator.

Works Cited

Ambrosini, Richard. *Conrad's Fiction as Critical Discourse*. Cambridge: Cambridge University Press, 1991

Bakhtin, M. M. *The Dialogic Imagination: Four Essays*. Ed. Michael Holquist. Tr. Caryl Emerson and Michael Holquist. Austin: University of Texas Press, 1982

Berthoud, Jacques. *Joseph Conrad: The Major Phase*. Cambridge: Cambridge University Press, 1978

———. 'Conrad and the sea'. Introduction. *The Nigger of the 'Narcissus'*. Ed. Jacques Berthoud. Oxford: Oxford University Press, 1984, pp. vii–xxvi

Bullough, Edward. 'Psychical distance'. 1912. In *Aesthetics: Lectures and Essays*. Ed. Elizabeth M. Wilkinson. Stanford: Stanford University Press, 1957, pp. 124–45

Cave, Terence. *Recognitions: A Study in Poetics*. Oxford: Clarendon Press, 1988

Cohn, Dorrit. *Transparent Minds: Narrative Modes for Presenting Consciousness in Fiction*. Princeton: Princeton University Press, 1978

Conrad, Joseph. *The Nigger of the 'Narcissus'*. 1897. Ed. Jacques Berthoud. Oxford: Oxford University Press, 1984
——. *'Heart of Darkness' and Other Tales*. Ed. Cedric Watts. Oxford: Oxford University Press, 1990
——. *Lord Jim, A Tale*. 1900. Ed. John Batchelor. Oxford: Oxford University Press, 1983
——. *Nostromo*. 1904. Ed. Keith Carabine. Oxford: Oxford University Press, 1984
——. *Under Western Eyes*. 1911. Ed. Jeremy Hawthorn. Oxford: Oxford University Press, 1983
Erdinast-Vulcan, Daphna. *Joseph Conrad and the Modern Temper*. Oxford: Clarendon Press, 1991
Genette, Gérard. *Narrative Discourse*. Oxford: Blackwell, 1980
Guerard, Albert J. *Conrad the Novelist*. Cambridge, MA: Harvard University Press, 1958
Hawthorn, Jeremy. *Joseph Conrad: Narrative Technique and Ideological Commitment*. London: Arnold, 1990
Henricksen, Bruce. *Nomadic Voices: Conrad and the Subject of Narrative*. Urbana: University of Illinois Press, 1992
Kayser, Wolfgang. *Das sprachliche Kunstwerk*. 1948. Berne: Francke Verlag, 1971
Lothe, Jakob. *Conrad's Narrative Method*. Oxford: Clarendon Press, 1989
Madsen, Peter. 'Modernitet og melankoli: Fortaelling, diskurs og identitet i Joseph Conrads *Mörkets hjerte*' ['Modernity and melancholy: narration, discourse, and identity in "Heart of Darkness"']. In *Fortaelling og erfaring*. Ed. O. B. Andersen *et al*. Aarhus: Aarhus University Press, 1988, pp. 97–118 (English version: *Conrad in Scandinavia*. Ed. Jakob Lothe. New York: Columbia University Press, 1995, pp. 127–54)
Miller, J. Hillis. *Fiction and Repetition: Seven English Novels*. Oxford: Blackwell, 1982
Najder, Zdzislaw. *Joseph Conrad: A Chronicle*. Tr. Halina Carroll-Najder. New Brunswick, NJ: Rutgers University Press; Cambridge: Cambridge University Press, 1983
Stanzel, Franz K. *A Theory of Narrative*. Cambridge: Cambridge University Press, 1986
Todorov, Tzvetan. *Introduction to Poetics*. Tr. Richard Howard. Brighton: Harvester, 1981
Trotter, David. *The English Novel in History: 1895–1920*. London: Routledge, 1993
Watt, Ian. *Conrad in the Nineteenth Century*. Berkeley: University of California Press, 1979; London: Chatto & Windus, 1980
Watts, Cedric. *A Preface to Conrad*. 2nd edn. London: Longman, 1993

Conrad, then, never wrote a true short story, a matter of two or three pages of minutely considered words, ending with a smack . . . with what the French call a *coup de canon*. His stories were always what for lack of a better phrase one has to call "long-short" stories. For these the form is practically the same as that of the novel. Or, to avoid the implication of saying that there is only one form for the novel, it would be better to put it that the form of long-short stories may vary as much as may the form for novels. The short story of Maupassant, of Tchekhov or even of the late O. Henry is practically stereotyped—the introduction of a character in a word or two, a word or two for atmosphere, a few paragraphs for story, and then, click! a sharp sentence that flashes the illumination of the idea over the whole.

This Conrad—and for the matter of that, the writer—never so much as attempted, either apart or in collaboration. The reason for this lies in all that is behind the mystic word "justification." Before everything a story must convey a sense of inevitability: that which happens in it must seem to be the only thing that could have happened. Of course a character may cry, "If I had then acted differently how different everything would now be." The problem of the author is to make his then action the only action that character could have taken. It must be inevitable, because of his character, because of his ancestry, because of past illness or on account of the gradual coming together of the thousand small circumstances by which Destiny, who is inscrutable and august, will push us into one certain predicament. Let us illustrate:

In rendering your long friendship with, and ultimate bitter hostility towards, your neighbour Mr Slack, who had a greenhouse painted with Cox's aluminium paint, you will, if you wish to get yourself in with the scrupulousness of a Conrad, have to provide yourself, in the first place, with an ancestry at least as far back as your grandparents. To account for your own stability of character and physical robustness you will have to give yourself two dear old grandparents in a lodge at the gates of a great nobleman: if necessary you will have to give them a brightly polished copper kettle simmering on a spotless hob, with silhouettes on each side of the mantel: in order to account for the lamentable procedure of your daughter Millicent you must provide yourself with an actress or gipsy-grandmother. Or at least with a French one. This grandmother will have lived, unfortunately unmarried, with some one of eloquence— possibly with the great Earl-Prime Minister at whose gates is situated the humble abode of your other grandparents—at any rate she will have lived with some one from whom you will have inherited your eloquence. From her will have descended the artistic gifts to which the reader will owe your admirable autobiographic novel.

If you have any physical weakness, to counterbalance the robustness of your other grandparents, you will provide your mother, shortly before your birth, with an attack of typhoid fever, due to a visit to Venice in company with your father, who was a gentleman's courier in the family in which your mother was a lady's maid. Your father, in order to be a courier, will have had, owing to his illegitimacy, to live abroad in very poor circumstances. The very poor circumstances will illustrate the avarice of his statesman father—an avarice which will have descended to you in the shape of that carefulness in money matters that, reacting on the detrimental tendencies inherited by Millicent from her actress-grandmother, so lamentably influences your daughter's destiny.

And of course there will have to be a great deal more than that, always supposing you to be as scrupulous as was Conrad in this matter of justification. For Conrad—and for the matter of that the writer—was never satisfied that he had really and sufficiently got his characters in; he was never convinced that he had convinced the reader; this accounting for the great lengths of some of his books. He never introduced a character, however subsidiary, without providing that character with ancestry and hereditary characteristics, or at least with home surroundings—always supposing that character had any influence on the inevitability of the story. Any policeman who arrested any character must be "justified", because the manner

54

in which he effected the arrest, his mannerisms, his vocabulary and his voice, might have a permanent effect on the psychology of the prisoner. The writer remembers Conrad using almost those very words during the discussion of the plot of "The Secret Agent."

This method, unless it is very carefully handled, is apt to have the grave defect of holding a story back very considerably. You must as a rule bring the biography of a character in only after you have introduced the character; yet, if you introduce a policeman to make an arrest the rendering of his biography might well retard the action of an exciting point in the story. . . . It becomes then your job to arrange that the very arresting of the action is an incitement of interest in the reader, just as, if you serialise a novel, you take care to let the words *"to be continued in our next"* come in at as harrowing a moment as you can contrive.

And of course the introducing of the biography of a character may have the great use of giving contrast to the tone of the rest of the book. . . . Supposing that in your history of your affair with Mr. Slack you think that the note of your orderly middle-class home is growing a little monotonous, it would be very handy if you could discover that Mr. Slack had a secret, dipsomaniacal wife, confined in a country cottage under the care of a rather criminal old couple; with a few pages of biography of that old couple you could give a very pleasant relief to the sameness of your narrative. In that way the sense of reality is procured.

MARTIN TUCKER ON SYMBOLIC LANGUAGE

Conrad's method in *Heart of Darkness* was to weave a tapestry of many complexities through his peculiar use of symbolic language. Symbols in Conrad are not given at one time fully; the reader gets the fullness of a Conradian symbol in stages, in voices heard and reheard with the phrase altered but the tone kept to the same pitch. In *Heart of Darkness* the word inscrutable is used repeatedly, in different circumstances to describe both character and setting; Conrad is suggesting the difficulty of the mystery of character, perhaps of the meaning of the universe. Kurtz's African mistress, who is described as larger than life, a woman of immense stature, is also, in a key scene, called inscrutable. By this method of repetition, Conrad establishes a mood and consciousness deeper than the formally symbolic. The reference to "pilgrims" is another example of his method—the quest for greed (in pursuit of ivory) is thrown shockingly into association with Kurtz's earlier status as a missionary of technological progress, and with the dedication associated with zealots. The three stations Marlow must cross suggest the Christian Stations of the Cross, paths of pain and agony that must be traversed to reach a peace and understanding, and a fulfillment of one's appointed place on earth. Conrad's grim satire on this point is evidenced by the hyperbolic statements the manager of the Central Station makes, among them this one: "Each station should be like a beacon on the road towards better things, a centre for trade, of course, but also for humanising, improving, instructing."

An excellent example of the integrated functions of this interweaving may be seen in the use Conrad makes of clothing. On an obvious level, Marlow sees two women knitting in the anteroom of the Great Company in Brussels (which he describes as the "whited sepulchre city"). They are "guarding the door of Darkness" and "knitting black wool in a warm pall," because "not half, by a long way of those who shipped out to Africa ever came back to Europe." The company is responsible for many deaths through its mistreatment of African natives. Also because of its ruthless drive for profits, the Company is willing to subject its employees to a brutalizing climate many of them cannot withstand.

The dress code, and lack of it, suggest another part of the meaning of the story. The Company accountant, who is always carefully groomed, is also inhuman when it comes to the groans of sick and dying men. Such noises "distract" the accountant from attention to his work. On the surface, the accountant seems a butt of Conrad's satire, for surely a man who values appearance above concern for humanity is not an object of admiration. Yet Conrad also suggests that the accountant keeps order. His way of dressing is a symbol of that order: he does not succumb to the "great demoralisation of the land."

To sustain order, then, seems to imply that certain cold, unfeeling, rigid lines of conduct must be observed. Otherwise one is led to the anarchy of dress—and of conduct—of the harlequin. Yet the harlequin, foolish as he is, is sympathetic to Marlow because of the unwavering loyalty the harlequin holds to Kurtz. At the end of the story, the harlequin is seen disappearing into the jungle to find a new habitation, because, like Kurtz, he has withdrawn from the civilized European world.

Conrad carefully places the accountant in the Outer Station, where things are seen from the outside, where order is imposed from without. The harlequin is, significantly, placed in the Inner Station, where order must come from within oneself, since all external authority, that of "civilization" anyway, has disappeared. Conrad convinces the reader that the harlequin must forsake his place in Western society if he is to continue, honestly, his unconventional life. Conversely, the accountant will never experience the depth of passion known by Kurtz, the harlequin, and their like.

The accountant's range of experience is also more restricted and narrow than that of Marlow, who has at least "peeped over the edge" in his meeting with Kurtz. The accountant does his job, and for him his way of life is rewarding: he is not aware of what he may be missing. But, then he has never gone beyond the Outer Station.

Images of light and darkness also provide their shade of meaning to the story. There is plenty of "light" at the Outer Station, but it is a light that does not penetrate into the center of things. At the Inner Station, the heart of darkness, Marlow finds a glimmer of understanding. Sound and silence also accompany the journey:

> Going up that river was like traveling back to the earliest beginnings of the world, when vegetation rioted on the earth and the big trees were kings. An empty stream,

a great silence, and an impenetrable forest. . . . It was the stillness of an implacable force brooding over an inscrutable intention.

CEDRIC T. WATTS ON COVERT PLOTS

Conrad was a master of the covert plot. Various of his novels and tales are characterised by the presence within the main narrative of smaller or larger plot-sequences which are so subtly and obliquely presented, with elisions or hiatuses, that they may be overlooked at the first or even second reading; indeed, some readers may never see them at all but may only have the feeling that some narrative enigma has been posed and left unresolved. When once the covert plot is perceived, various consequences ensue. The narrative as a whole is seen to be more intelligently artful in its exposition; the work becomes more ironic and certain themes gain richer presentation. Generally the mode of concealment of elements of the plot is that we see through the eyes or "over the shoulder" of a protagonist or narrator who is being deceived or circumvented and who is slow to perceive, if he perceives at all, the web that others are weaving around him. The covert plots of Conrad are therefore covert in two senses: concealed from a central observer, and largely concealed (at least at the first reading) from the reader.

The elision or withholding of logical connections preoccupies Conrad the story-teller as it preoccupies Conrad the descriptive artist. He developed to sophisticated extremes the art of "delayed decoding" (Ian Watt's phrase) in descriptive passages: he presents the effect while withholding or delaying the knowledge of the cause; and the result is that the event gains in vividness of impact while initially seeming strange, random or absurd, a quality diminished but seldom erased by our subsequent perception of the rational explanation. There are hundreds of possible examples, including the presentation of the death of Marlow's helmsman in *Heart of Darkness*, the explosion of the coal-gas in "Youth," and the onset of rain in *The Shadow-Line*. . . .

In *Heart of Darkness*, as I have shown in more detail previously,[5] the covert plot is the manager's plot to ensure the demise of Kurtz, his rival for promotion, by wrecking the steamer and delaying its repair, so that Kurtz's relief arrives too late. As Marlow tells his tale, he is in process of perceiving the full extent of the manager's plot: "I did not see the real significance of that wreck at once. I fancy I see it now, but I am not sure—not at all. Certainly the affair was too stupid—when I think of it—to be altogether natural. Still. . . ."[6] The manager estimates that the repair (which will be delayed by the lack of rivets) will take as long as three months. Marlow says: "I flung out of his hut. . . . He was a chattering idiot. Afterwards I took it back when it was borne in upon me startlingly with what extreme nicety he had estimated the time requisite for the 'affair.'"[7] Consequently, by the time the steamer reaches the inner station, Kurtz is deranged and dying.

The covert plot, when perceived, increases greatly the tale's ironies: among other things, it makes a sardonic comment on the belief of political Darwinians that the white man has a God-given right to invade and colonise tropical lands; for it shows that morally the Europeans, who treacherously scheme against their fellows, are no better and indeed probably worse (because of their hypocrisy) than those they purport to civilise. (We may recall Conrad's scorn for Lord Salisbury's view that the "living nations," such as Great Britain, must inevitably encroach upon and cut up the "dying.") If harmony between creature and his environment is a goal of the evolutionary process, that harmony has been attained not by the restless white men, who, with the exception of the abnormally healthy manager, tend to succumb to illness within months of arrival in Africa, but by the natives who so energetically paddle their canoe through the surf: "They shouted, sang; their bodies streamed with perspiration, they had faces like grotesque masks—these chaps; but they had bone, muscle, a wild vitality, an intense energy of movement, that was as natural and true as the surf along their coast. They wanted no excuse for being there. They were a great comfort to look at."[8]

But, if the covert plot thus contributes importantly to the tale's themes, the reader may well ask why it is covert instead of overt. The answer is that by the elliptical presentation of the manager's plot against Kurtz, Conrad can have his cake and eat it: he has the best of both possibilities. Through the elliptical presentation, which initially conceals the plot's logic from the reader, Conrad is able to preserve that important initial impression that Marlow has entered a region of irrationality, nightmare, and absurdity, a region of crass purposelessness: the theme of the futility of imperialism is thus emphasised, while the more general theme of the perils of crossing the threshold from the familiar to the unknown is maintained. When we eventually, in retrospect, see the covert plot, the theme of futile activity is modified by our recognition that some activity in the Congo may indeed be purposeful and effective—but since it is maliciously competitive activity by a European, it still supports the criticism of imperialism and the warnings about the dangers of the unknown. As Africa ambushes Europeans, so the narrative ambushes readers.

What commentators on Conrad have so far overlooked is that the covert plots and narrative obliquities of the later works have been boldly anticipated in Conrad's first novel, *Almayer's Folly*. As in *Heart of Darkness*, the overlooked material in *Almayer's Folly* concerns a treacherous scheme by one trader to defeat another in an exotic, remote region to which both have come from afar.

Notes

5. Cedric Watts, *Conrad's "Heart of Darkness": A Critical and Contextual Discussion* (Mursia International, Milan, 1977), pp. 82–5; also *Conradiana*, vol. VII (1975), pp. 137–43.

6. *Youth*, p. 72.

7. *Youth*, p. 75.

8. *Youth*, p. 61.

MARK WOLLAEGER ON SKEPTICISM AND THE SEARCH FOR GOD IN MAN

Literature has registered God's disappearance in a variety of ways.[27] In Dickens, God's presence remains accessible beyond the human labyrinth of the city for those who have eyes to see. George Eliot, in the well-known anecdote of her conversation with F. W. H. Myers, showed greater equanimity in accepting a world whose transcendental sanctions had not receded but vanished. Of God, immortality, and duty she "pronounced, with terrible earnestness, how inconceivable was the *first*, how unbelievable the *second*, and yet how peremptory and absolute the *third*." Beyond equanimity, Lawrence exhibits almost complete indifference when Birkin heralds the new secularism in a dependent clause.[28]

There is a certain belatedness in Conrad's response to the *deus absconditus*, and in this respect he is closer to Dickens than to George Eliot or Lawrence. The shock that reverberates through his work is immediate, emotional, and anguished—like Marlow's when he discovers that Kurtz has escaped:

> The fact is I was completely unnerved by a sheer blank fright, pure abstract terror, unconnected with any distinct shape of physical danger. What made this emotion so overpowering was— how shall I define it?—the moral shock I received, as if something altogether monstrous, intolerable to thought and odious to the soul, had been thrust upon me unexpectedly. (*HD* 141)

I take Marlow's anxiety and terror as a synecdoche for Conrad's own response to finding the heavens empty. But well before Marlow's shock over Kurtz's absence, the departure of God in "Heart of Darkness" is closely linked to Marlow's journey toward Kurtz. When Marlow begins his narration with a rather weak attempt to distinguish between British colonialism and the more brutally rapacious Belgian variety in the Congo Free State, his argument suggests the need for what sounds like a form of primitive religion: "What redeems it is the idea only. An idea at the back of it; not a sentimental pretence but an idea; and an unselfish belief in the idea— something you can set up, and bow down before, and offer a sacrifice to . . ." (*HD* 51). Kurtz, who comes to be seen as a supernatural being by the natives, practices only a selfish religion, perhaps even a religion *of* the self. Nevertheless, from the amoral hypocrisy of the company manager Marlow turns "mentally to Kurtz for relief—positively for relief" (*HD* 138). Although Kurtz has plummeted from the culmination of European Liberalism to atavistic savagery, Marlow still prefers the assertion of some form of conviction to a skeptical emptying out of all beliefs. . . .

Before discovering Kurtz's emptiness, Marlow fixates on the desire to hear his voice as a defense, like the shelter afforded by the book of seamanship, against the frightening blankness and silence of the wilderness. Unsettled, at one point Marlow suddenly breaks from his monologue to address his audience more directly, as if challenging them to respond. The rhetorical gesture instantly conjures the social connection whose absence he feared in the wilderness: "how can you imagine what particular region of the first ages a man's untrammelled feet may take him into by the way of solitude— utter solitude without a policeman—by the way of silence— utter silence, where no warning voice of a kind neighbour can be heard whispering of public opinion?" (*HD* 116). The passage assumes that an investment in authority, whether the disciplinary effect of the police or of language, acts as a defense against a kind of "natural" atavism. It also brings out the extent to which Conrad's work is suffused with the fear of loneliness.[31] The narrator of *Under Western Eyes* remarks of Razumov: "Who knows what true loneliness is—not the conventional word, but the naked terror? . . . No human being could bear a steady view of moral solitude without going mad" (*UWE* 39). Such fear is basic to the psychology of skepticism: "As long as God exists, I am not alone. And couldn't the other suffer the fate of God?" This train of thought leads to the hypothesis that "the philosophical problem of the other [is] the trace or scar of the departure of God."[32] Descending from the divine to the human, the problem of the other plays out our anxieties about knowing and being known. For Marlow, Kurtz becomes that other, yet he occupies an unsettling position between the human and something beyond "the threshold of the invisible" (*HD* 151).

Marlow first becomes obsessed with the consolation of Kurtz's voice when his native helmsman is killed by a spear thrown from the riverbank. Whatever his deficiencies, the helmsman had carried out one of the most valuable duties a character in Conrad can perform—like Singleton, he had steered. His death persuades Marlow that Kurtz also must have died in the attack: "I couldn't have felt more of lonely desolation somehow, had I been robbed of a belief or had missed my destiny in life" (*HD* 114). A potential substitution for the helmsman ("And couldn't the other suffer the fate of God?"), Kurtz presents himself to Marlow only as a voice, and the promise of this voice comes to represent the sheltering and sheltered intention he so desires. But before experiencing the deep duplicity of Kurtz's "gift of expression . . . the pulsating stream of light, or the deceitful flow from the heart of an impenetrable darkness" (*HD* 113–14), Marlow comes face to face with a parody of his own desire to believe in Kurtz in the figure of the Russian harlequin, who babbles with the enthusiasm of a disciple of Reverend Moon: "'I tell you,' he cried, 'this man has enlarged my mind,' He opened his arms wide, staring at me with his little blue eyes that were perfectly round" (*HD* 125). Although his own loyalty will run deeper, at this moment Marlow "does not envy him his devotion to Kurtz" (*HD* 127).

Marlow's preference for the nightmare of Kurtz over that of the trading company eventually assumes the form of an ambivalent discipleship. Like a priest presiding over the relics of a saint, Marlow takes care to alter the text that will perpetuate an idealized version of Kurtz by tearing off the savage postscript to the "Suppression of Savage Customs." Lying to the Intended, Marlow continues to protect an ideal image of Kurtz, again by paying tribute only to what Kurtz originally intended. The anxious effort to suppress publicity about Kurtz's savage customs is of a piece with Marlow's lame defense of English colonialism in expressing a longing for the sort of certainty once provided by religion.

Hoping for something human in the wilderness, Marlow finds the Russian—a blithering zealot—and Kurtz. But Kurtz has withdrawn into a world of his own creation. From the Russian Marlow learns that "'you don't talk with that man—you listen to him'" (*HD* 123). Even before meeting him Marlow remarks, "I had never imagined him as doing, you know, but as discoursing" (*HD* 113). Yet when Marlow hears about Kurtz's "monologues," he considers that the Russian's devotion may be "about the most dangerous thing in every way he had come upon so far" (*HD* 127). In his climactic showdown with Kurtz just beyond the circle of his worshipers, Marlow understands these monologues as the expression of a man whose "intelligence," though "perfectly clear," was "concentrated . . . upon himself with horrible intensity" (*HD* 144). Bracketed within Marlow's first encounters with the Russian and Kurtz is his horrified discovery that what seemed "round carved balls" ornamenting fence posts are actually "symbolic" heads on stakes with all of the faces but one turned in toward Kurtz's house. The heads literalize the potential violence of moral skepticism; the human other has become purely instrumental. Those gazing inward reflect Kurtz's own self-absorption while the one turned outward beckons, like the forest, to Marlow, who ultimately manages to establish the connection he has been seeking all along.

The Russian only listens to Kurtz (and consequently is "filled" and "occupied" by him); Marlow, when faced with the necessity of preventing Kurtz's return to the midnight rites, *talks* him back to the hut. Dialogue emerges here as an antidote to the self-enclosure of monologue. Yet in narrating his story to the audience on the *Nellie*, Marlow reexperiences the danger to which Kurtz has succumbed. To his auditors Marlow had "for a long time" already become, as Kurtz was to Marlow, "no more to us than a voice" (*HD* 83). Marlow himself underlines the problem when, in the passage that begins this chapter, he declares the impossibility of ever communicating "the life-sensation" of his experience in Africa: "We live, as we dream—alone." Providing Marlow with an audience to shape his utterance, Conrad aims to transform a potential prison house of language into what Henry James called "a noble sociability of vision."[33] The breadth of this society, however, is quite limited. "Be civil," someone interrupts: to the extent that dialogue between Englishmen becomes a synecdoche for all civilized discourse, Marlow is.

Although dialogue holds the potential to undo the solipsism of monologue, the fear that language may inevitably fail to communicate whatever is most important runs deep in Conrad. "Your own reality", Marlow claims in his praise of work, is inaccessible to others: "they only see the mere show, and never can tell what it really means" (*HD* 85). For Bakhtin true dialogic structure emerges from what Keats called "negative capability," the capacity to understand all points of view from the inside out and the willingness to accord each an equal say. The monologic is associated with the Romantic cult of the personality and its tendency to objectify whatever cannot be absorbed into its own perspective.[34] Kurtz has long been recognized as the epitome of Romantic individualism,[35] and in "Heart of Darkness" Conrad dramatizes, in the relationships between Kurtz and Marlow and between Marlow and the inscribed audience, the danger of the collapse of the dialogic into the monologic. Marlow, by withdrawing his hesitating foot, preserves the capacity to maintain a dialogue with his audience—though admittedly (if we exclude the chorus of critical response) a rather one-sided one. In *Nostromo* the collapse into monological authority will be associated with political and physical violence, the ferocious imposition of a single will. Although Kurtz's savagery anticipates this theme, in "Heart of Darkness" Conrad ultimately seems less concerned with the political critique of colonialism that dominates the first section of the novella than with the more narrowly social and literary problem that Marlow's narration may become purely self-reflexive.

By its very nature, however, language cannot become a wholly private set of dream symbols. If, as Wittgenstein asserted, a word's meaning is its use, "use" also implies the history of its use: maverick usage does not necessarily assign a new (and possibly private) meaning to a word.[36] "The fantasy of a private language," according to Cavell, "can be understood as an attempt to account for, and protect, our separateness, our unknowingness, our unwillingness or incapacity either to know or to be known."[37] Marlow's rather defensive outbursts against his audience are suggestive of a conflicted attempt to confront his own sense of isolation. In *Lord Jim*, where Jim reaches "the secret fount of [Marlow's] egotism," the ambivalent desire to share and withhold through narration is played out in the disruptions and dislocations of narrative chronology. Here the emphasis falls less on the problem of other minds per se than on the capacity of Marlow's narration to rescue "the shade of the original Kurtz," the one committed to humanitarian ideals, from the encompassing darkness (*HD* 147).

Watching Kurtz die, Marlow feels "as though a veil had been rent" (*HD* 149), but the unveiling only leads to an undecidable question. Kurtz may or may not have been able to reaffirm the validity of ethical categories in his dying words: he whispers, "at some image, at some vision"—an image from memory or a vision of certitudes beyond the human? Deathbed scenes in Victorian literature, one critic has suggested, may function in part to suppress such uncertainties: "When the heart is so strongly moved, the skeptical intellect is silenced."[38] The absence of the sentimental response to skepticism in Kurtz's last moments only heightens the indeterminacy of what we are to make of his experience ("the horror, the horror"?) and so intensifies the skeptical confusion inspired in Marlow and the reader. Has Kurtz pierced to the moral occult, or is Marlow again turning to him for relief where none is warranted?

Notes

27. The classic treatment of this theme is Miller's *The Disappearance of God*, which analyzes "heroic attempts to recover immanence in a world of transcendence" (p. 15).

28. In *Bleak House*, Tulkinghorn, much to his misfortune, does not have eyes to see. As he walks out on the leads, Tulkinghorn's absorption in the futile legal documents on his writing table blinds him to the signs that portend his own death: "The time was when men as knowing as Mr Tulkinghorn would walk on turret-tops in the starlight, and look up into the sky to read their fortunes there." *Bleak House*, 631. The Eliot anecdote is quoted in Haight, *George Eliot*, 464. In *Women in Love*, Gerald asks, ". . . you mean if there isn't the

woman, there's nothing?", to which Birkin replies, "Pretty well that—seeing there's no God" (p. 51).

31. For a sustained treatment of this theme, see Gillon, *The Eternal Solitary*.

32. Cavell, *The Claim of Reason*, 470.

33. James, *Notes on Novelists*, 351.

34. Bakhtin, *Problems of Dostoevsky's Poetics*, 9–13, 27.

35. For the classic reading of "Heart of Darkness" as an expression of "the disenchantment of our culture with culture itself," see Trilling, "On the Teaching of Modern Literature," in his *Beyond Culture*. He elaborates the argument, now cast as the rebellion of the Romantic self against the inauthenticity of society, in *Sincerity and Authenticity*, 106–11, 133.

36. On the mind's resistance to the private redefinition of language, see Quigley, "Wittgenstein's Philosophizing and Literary Philosophizing" (1988), esp. 220–21.

37. Cavell, *The Claim of Reason*, 369.

38. Houghton, *The Victorian Frame of Mind*, 277.

DANIEL C. MELNICK ON MORALITY AND THE ROLE OF THE READER

What exactly was the novelist's view of the social and moral condition of human life? The difficulty of answering the question grows out of the conflict between Conrad's basic yet sometimes only suggested pessimism and his explicit affirmations. His finest novels lead the reader into a world of "vain and floating appearance," into a symbolic heart of darkness where he is made to doubt the reality and effective value of all social and personal order. Yet, in the face of the evoked moral disintegration, Conrad's narrators often affirm a morality of decency and fidelity, of "human solidarity." This contradiction between pessimism and affirmation is a complex and integral part of our experience of reading the novels

The sense of Conrad's values which I want to explore is that the basis of his deepest moral commitment is located in neither affirmation nor pessimism, but in Conrad's reliance on the reader's ability to use his own imagination, a reliance which Conrad often voiced. In the novels, the idealist, the steeled cynic, and the human stoic are each maimed or destroyed by the anarchy, the mystery, and the extremities of fate which constitute the malevolent nature of the reality Conrad envisions. Only the observing eyes of the reader and in a sense those of narrators survive the ruin of human experience; human vision alone endures. Conrad's finest novels subtly project this crucial reliance on and respect for the reader who is able imaginatively to face and judge disintegrating experience. . . .

Conrad's fiction calls upon the reader to take up the responsibility for moral exploration and judgment that arises from the experience of reading such work; the narratives are by design lifelike, both in assaulting the reader's temperament and expectations, and in offering him an opportunity to explore and affirm his own capacity for human awareness. The sort of moral heroism Conrad hopes fiction can draw from the reader is summoned up in him by the novel which stirs to life his capacity to face and judge a world where traditional human order seems to fall apart. Conrad's art compels the reader to place his own capacity for self-examination at the center of his imaginative experience. In *Nostromo*, for example, the narrative's complexity projects the shattering tension between human aspiration and reality with its subverting impact on Decoud, Mrs. Gould, and each provisional narrative center of perception; the value and meaning of the novel depend finally on the insight, the independent judgment, and the heightened imaginative and moral rigor of the response which the assaulting flux of such form draws from the reader. In the following pages, I explore the ways in which *Nostromo* and *Heart of Darkness*, two of Conrad's finest novels, challenge the reader to find meaning and transcendence in his own investment of creative energy. In the visions these two novels offer, the survival of the human spirit depends on the awakened imagination of the reader, on his acceptance of a crucial and difficult place at the center of the form of the novels. Conrad's strategy is that the fiction's meaning becomes the engagement and revelation of the reader's own sense of human possibility, and that strategy underlies the aim and value of his finest works. . . .

Let me turn again to *Heart of Darkness*, and more fully and closely identify the strategy and morality of Conrad's imagination in it. Here, in a work written at the turn of the century and four years before *Nostromo*, the order—the controlling illusion—of civilization seems to disintegrate, leaving the reader with a vision of anarchic darkness in the mind of the central 'anti-hero' Kurtz and menacing, as we saw, the mind of the central narrator, Marlow. The journey Marlow takes, of course, echoes in part Conrad's own Congo trip, his physically and spiritually exhausting final command; and in his subsequent writing career, Conrad was obsessed by the vision of darkness embodied in Marlow's journey. The two central consciousnesses the reader encounters in the work are not made merely nihilistic by their experience of the Congo darkness. On the contrary, to consider Kurtz before we focus again on Marlow, he meets his final destruction as a sort of idealist.

Kurtz entered the Congo service with the "highest" ideals and brilliant qualifications. He is motivated by a sense of pontifical superiority to the 'savage' nature of Africa and Africans. Experiencing the seemingly absolute indifference of the African social and physical 'darkness,' Kurtz's will knows no bounds; and it grows monstrous on its abstract fare of Western imperialistic ideals. A man of destructive illusions, he is without any realistic perception of human decencies or of the human condition before him. Of African natives, he thus can write "exterminate the brutes"; he has himself been worshipped in a moral obscenity as a savage god; and he attempts to act like one. Kurtz's experience is a symbolic revelation of the passionate destructiveness beneath the surface of Western ideals (to which he is committed), and his revelation of evil is designed to implicate the reader and indeed civilization itself. Conrad does not directly present the heart of darkness within Kurtz; he suggests and symbolizes its anarchic existence by means of its effect on Marlow. Yet Kurtz does at one point directly and profoundly speak out to involve us; that is when he himself becomes conscious of the meaning of his experience. Kurtz's pontifical voice is hollow and without self-awareness except for the single self-condemning insight of his final utterance: "the horror, the horror." This is as far as Conrad takes us into the particular center of Kurtz's experience.

Kurtz's fate reveals the destructive reality beneath the apparent order in human experience. In contrast, Marlow's narration reveals the vulnerability of a man's personal and communal identity to that inner reality. Marlow is a thoughtful man, sensitive to both the good and the evil in his and other men's acts, a truthful observer, a dedicated mariner. It is through his eyes that the reader encounters Kurtz, through Marlow's narrative of his journey up the Congo to contact Kurtz on behalf of their imperialist employers. From the start, the reader is struck by the honesty, maturity, and imaginative sensitivity of Marlow's observations. Blinded by neither pettiness nor idealism he perceives the reality of the human condition before him—whether it be the "insanity" of the anchored French man-of-war shooting into the African continent, the dying African slaves in the grove of death, the human restraint of his hungry cannibal crew, or the unrestrained meanness of the European pilgrims in the Congo.

The values of duty and decency which are sometimes said to sustain Marlow would be shallow and vulnerable if they were not the outgrowth of his maturity and truthfulness of *perception*. When, for example, his decency compels him to tell Kurtz's beloved a merciful "white lie," it is not out of habitual morality; it is because the "altogether too dark" spectre of Kurtz and his final whisper possess and mortify his imagination. Marlow's painful and incisive perception is that this illusion-bound woman could not understand or accommodate the knowledge of Kurtz's last words that he, Marlow, labors under and endures. Marlow's mature decency is based finally on the quality of his imagination which, in a desperate paradox, is also the basis of his final awareness of the darkness at the heart of human experience.

As he nears Kurtz's station in the novel, the moral depth and emotional maturity of Marlow's identity as an observer are severely tested. On first hearing of Kurtz's idealistic and authoritative voice, Marlow identifies with him; and as he penetrates deeper into the darkness of the Congo, he sustains his sense of himself in part by means of that sympathetic identification. When he gains his final knowledge of Kurtz's actual corruption Marlow says: "it is his extremity I seemed to have lived through," an extremity revealing a negation at the heart of human ideals and the human voice itself—that is to say, communication itself.

Marlow's attempt to communicate this self-challenging, indeed self-disintegrating insight is the crucial source of the work's assaulting power. As he emphasized the affirmative value of Kurtz's sole *voicing* of the nature of his situation, Marlow is actually suggesting the embattled power of his own most significant qualities, the perceptive sympathy and severe honesty of his narration. Without those qualities his story would be the simple and insignificant one of the single-minded fortitude of a mariner on a dangerous mission. At times, the tone of the narrative does in fact seem to mix the desperately rigid piety of his appeal to simple values ("faithfulness" and "devotion to work") with his obsessive anxiety about the ominous nature of his experience. Both the piety and the anxiety are, however, defenses against the inner heart of darkness, his own, Kurtz's, and mankind's. The process of self-defense in him accompanies that of self-discovery.

Both processes are clear in the following quotation; Marlow here seeks terms which can voice his self-challenging perception of Kurtz.

> "Since I had peeped over the edge myself, I understand better the meaning of his stare, that could not see the flame of the candle, but was wide enough to embrace the whole universe, piercing enough to penetrate all the hearts that beat in the darkness. He had summed up—he had judged. 'The horror.' ... [This cry] was an affirmation, a moral victory paid for by innumerable defeats, by abominable terrors, by abominable satisfactions."

Here the reader encounters a flux of ambiguity unlike any found in earlier novelists. The ambiguities of metaphor and tone are not fluidly, masterfully ironic, but desperately grasping and evasive. Marlow comprehends a stare "piercing enough to penetrate" to the heart of a darkness which is "evanescing," "mysterious," and "impenetrable." The anxiously ambiguous and evasive prose attempts to convey the dimensions of the menace and to heighten the sense of the risk and moral value of perception and judgment. Conrad's reader is placed in a position to observe both processes of self-defense and discovery at work in the narrative. That position is similar to, but far more strategic and self-conscious than, the symbolic position of the listener-narrator of the novel's frame. In essence, Conrad is placing us in a position to carry and affirm Marlow's imaginative viewpoint beyond the limits of his expression of it.

A key effect achieved here is that the reader himself is never made to perceive the central "horror" but only the husk of ambiguities surrounding and suggesting it, a husk of implication which the novel's framing narrator says characterizes Marlow's tales generally. That characteristic effect is the most significant feature of the novel itself; for not the particular horror in Kurtz but, instead, the act of penetrating and exploring a potential darkness in the self is the novel's subject and its informing symbol. Marlow's narrative offers the reader not a particular discovery but the form itself of discovery, the means which enable and indeed challenge him—with and beyond Marlow—to explore the abyss of the self. That form of discovery with the reader's imaginative penetration at its center makes *Heart of Darkness* a seminal and most forceful achievement in modern fiction.

The image of Marlow's journey of discovery is, then, a crucial and revealing one for the role of the reader himself who in imagination penetrates to the "heart of darkness," who comprehends both the achievement of Marlow's penetration and its limits, his defensive piety and obscurity. A refinement and extension of Marlow's role, the reader's final responsibility is to see the subversive and malevolent reality underlying both man's nature and his experience, to oppose to this his own consciousness, his capacity deeply to penetrate an ambiguous and menacing vision of experience, and so to affirm with Conrad the enduring power of that rich and courageous form of imagination. This reliance of the author on the reader to see beyond the negations of *Heart of Darkness* expresses the desperation of his view of life and art; the final effect of this desperation is to place the reader in the position of the novel's ultimate hero.

CHINUA ACHEBE ON CONRAD'S IMAGE OF AFRICA

Heart of Darkness projects the image of Africa as "the other world," the antithesis of Europe and therefore of civilization, a place where man's vaunted intelligence and refinement are finally mocked by triumphant bestiality. The book opens on the River Thames, tranquil, resting peacefully "at the decline of the day after ages of good service done to the race that peopled its banks." But the actual story will take place on the River Congo, the very antithesis of the Thames. The River Congo is quite decidedly not a River Emeritus. It has rendered no service and enjoys no old-age pension. We are told that "Going up that river was like travelling back to the earliest beginnings of the world."

Is Conrad saying then that these two rivers are very different, one good, the other bad? Yes, but that is not the real point. It is not the differentness that worries Conrad but the lurking hint of kinship, of common ancestry. For the Thames too "has been one of the dark places of the earth." It conquered its darkness, of course, and is now in daylight and at peace. But if it were to visit its primordial relative, the Congo, it would run the terrible risk of hearing grotesque echoes of its own forgotten darkness, and falling victim to an avenging recrudescence of the mindless frenzy of the first beginnings.

These suggestive echoes comprise Conrad's famed evocation of the African atmosphere in *Heart of Darkness*. In the final consideration his method amounts to no more than a steady, ponderous, fake-ritualistic repetition of two antithetical sentences, one about silence and the other about frenzy. We can inspect samples of this on pages 34 and 35 of the present edition: a) *It was the stillness of an implacable force brooding over an inscrutable intention* and b) *The steamer toiled alone slowly on the edge of a black and incomprehensible frenzy.* Of course there is a judicious change of adjective from time to time, so that instead of *inscrutable*, for example, you might have *unspeakable*, even plain *mysterious*, etc., etc.

The eagle-eyed English critic F. R. Leavis drew attention long ago to Conrad's "adjectival insistence upon inexpressible and incomprehensible mystery." That insistence must not be dismissed lightly, as many Conrad critics have tended to do, as a mere stylistic flaw; for it raises serious questions of artistic good faith. When a writer while pretending to record scenes, incidents and their impact is in reality engaged in inducing hypnotic stupor in his readers through a bombardment of emotive words and other forms of trickery, much more has to be at stake than stylistic felicity. Generally normal readers are well armed to detect and resist such underhand activity. But Conrad chose his subject well—one which was guaranteed not to put him in conflict with the psychological pre-disposition of his readers or raise the need for him to contend with their resistance. He chose the role of purveyor of comforting myths.

The most interesting and revealing passages in *Heart of Darkness* are, however, about people. I must crave the indulgence of my reader to quote almost a whole page from about the middle of the story when representatives of Europe in a steamer going down the Congo encounter the denizens of Africa.

> We were wanderers on a prehistoric earth, on an earth that wore the aspect of an unknown planet. We could have fancied ourselves the first of men taking possession of an accursed inheritance, to be subdued at the cost of profound anguish and of excessive toil. But suddenly as we struggled round a bend there would be a glimpse of rush walls, of peaked grass-roofs, a burst of yells, a whirl of black limbs, a mass of hands clapping, of feet stamping, of bodies swaying, of eyes rolling under the droop of heavy and motionless foliage. The steamer toiled

along slow on the edge of a black and incomprehensible frenzy. The prehistoric man was cursing us, praying to us, welcoming us—who could tell? We were cut off from the comprehension of our surroundings; we glided past like phantoms, wondering and secretly appalled, as sane men would be before an enthusiastic outbreak in a madhouse. We could not understand because we were too far and could not remember, because we were travelling in the night of first ages, of those ages that are gone, leaving hardly a sign—and no memories.

The earth seemed unearthly, We are accustomed to look upon the shackled form of a conquered monster, but there—there you could look at a thing monstrous and free. It was unearthly and the men were. . . . No they were not inhuman. Well you know that was the worst of it—this suspicion of their not being inhuman. It would come slowly to one. They howled and leaped and spun and made horrid faces, but what thrilled you was just the thought of their inhumanity—like yours—the thought of your remote kinship with this wild and passionate uproar. Ugly. Yes, it was ugly enough, but if you were man enough you would admit to yourself that there was in you just the faintest trace of a response to the terrible frankness of that noise, a dim suspicion of there being a meaning in it which you—you so remote from the night of first ages—could comprehend.

Herein lies the meaning of *Heart of Darkness* and the fascination it holds over the Western mind: "What thrilled you was just the thought of their humanity—like yours. . . . Ugly."

Having shown us Africa in the mass, Conrad then zeros in, half a page later, on a specific example, giving us one of his rare descriptions of an African who is no just limbs or rolling eyes.

And between whiles I had to look after the savage who was fireman. He was an improved specimen; he could fire up a vertical boiler. He was there below me and, upon my word, to look at him was as edifying as seeing a dog in a parody of breeches and a feather hat walking on his hind legs. A few months of training had done for that really fine chap. He squinted at the steam-gauge and at the water-gauge with an evident effort of intrepidity—and he had filed his teeth too, the poor devil, and the wool of his pate shaved into queer patterns, and three ornamental scars on each of his cheeks. He ought to have been clapping his hands and stamping his feet on the bank, instead of which he was hard at work, a thrall to strange witchcraft, full of improving knowledge.

As everybody knows, Conrad is a romantic on the side. He might not exactly admire savages clapping their hands and stamping their feet but they have at least the merit of being in their place, unlike this dog in a parody of breeches. For Conrad things[4] being in their place is of the utmost importance.

"Fine fellows—cannibals—in their place," he tells us pointedly. Tragedy begins when things leave their accustomed place, like Europe leaving its safe stronghold between the policeman and the baker to take a peep into the heart of darkness.

Before the story takes us into the Congo basin proper we are given this nice little vignette as an example of things in their place:

> Now and then a boat from the shore gave one a momentary contact with reality. It was paddled by black fellows. You could see from afar the white of their eyeballs glistening. They shouted, sang; their bodies streamed with perspiration; they had faces like grotesque masks— these chaps; but they had bone, muscle, a wild vitality, an intense energy of movement that was as natural and true as the surf along their coast. They wanted no excuse for being there, They were a great comfort to look at.

Towards the end of the story Conrad lavishes a whole page[5] quite unexpectedly on an African woman who has obviously been some kind of mistress to Mr. Kurtz and now presides (if

I may be permitted a little liberty)[6] like a formidable mystery over the inexorable imminence of his departure:

> She was savage and superb, wild-eyed and magnificent. . . . She stood looking at us without a stir and like the wilderness itself, with an air of brooding over an inscrutable purpose.

This Amazon is drawn in considerable detail, albeit of a predictable nature, for two reasons. First, she is in her place and so can win Conrad's special brand of approval and second, she fulfills a structural requirement of the story: a savage counterpart to the refined, European woman who will step forth to end the story:

> She came forward all in black with a pale head, floating toward me in the dusk. She was in mourning. . . . She took both my hands in hers and murmured, "I had heard you were coming." . . . She had a mature capacity for fidelity, or belief, or suffering.

The difference in the attitude of the novelist to these two women is conveyed in too many direct and subtle ways to need elaboration. But perhaps the most significant difference is the one implied in the author's bestowal of human expression to the one and the withholding of it from the other. It is clearly not part of Conrad's purpose to confer language on the "rudimentary souls" of Africa. In place of speech they made "a violent babble of uncouth sounds."[7] They "exchanged short grunting phrases" even among themselves. But most of the time they were too busy with their frenzy. There are two occasions in the book, however, when Conrad departs somewhat from his practice and confers speech, even English speech, on the savages. The first occurs when cannibalism gets the better of them:

> "Catch 'im" he snapped with a bloodshot widening of his eyes and a flash of sharp teeth—"catch 'im. Give 'im

to us." "To you, eh?" I asked; "what would you do with them?" "Eat 'im!" he said curtly. . . .

The other occasion was the famous announcement:

"Mistah Kurtz—he dead."

At first sight these instances might be mistaken for unexpected acts of generosity from Conrad. In reality they constitute some of his best assaults. In the case of the cannibals the incomprehensible grunts that had thus far served them for speech suddenly proved inadequate for Conrad's purpose of letting the European glimpse the unspeakable craving in their hearts. Weighing the necessity for consistency in the portrayal of the dumb brutes against the sensational advantages of securing their conviction by clear, unambiguous evidence issuing out of their own mouth, Conrad chose the latter. As for the announcement of Mr. Kurtz's death by the "insolent black head in the doorway" what better or more appropriate *finis* could be written to the horror story of that wayward child of civilization who willfully had given his soul to the powers of darkness and "taken a high seat amongst the devils of the land" than the proclamation of his physical death by the forces he had joined?

It might be contended, of course, that the attitude to the African in *Heart of Darkness* is not Conrad's but that of his fictional narrator, Marlow, and that far from endorsing it Conrad might indeed be holding it up to irony and criticism. Certainly Conrad appears to go to considerable pains to set up layers of insulation between himself and the moral universe of his history. He has, for example, a narrator behind a narrator. The primary narrator is Marlow but his account is given to us through the filter of a second, shadowy person. But if Conrad's intention is to draw a *cordon sanitaire*[8] between himself and the moral and psychological malaise of his narrator his care seems to me totally wasted because he neglects to hint however subtly or tentatively at an alternative frame of reference by which we may judge the actions and opinions of his characters. It would not have been beyond Conrad's power to make that provision if he had thought it necessary. Marlow seems to me to enjoy Conrad's complete confidence—a feeling reinforced by the close similarities between their two careers.

Marlow comes through to us not only as a witness of truth, but one holding those advanced and humane views appropriate to the English liberal tradition which required all Englishmen of decency to be deeply shocked by atrocities in Bulgaria or the Congo of King Leopold of the Belgians or wherever. . . .

The point of my observations should be quite clear by now, namely that Joseph Conrad was a thoroughgoing[9] racist. That this simple truth is glossed over in criticisms of his work is due to the fact that white racism against Africa is such a normal way of thinking that its manifestations go completely unremarked. Students of *Heart of Darkness* will often tell you that Conrad is concerned not so much with Africa as with the deterioration of one European mind caused by solitude and sickness. They will point out to you that Conrad is, if anything, less charitable to the Europeans in the story than he is to the natives, that the point of the story is to ridicule Europe's civilizing mission in Africa.[10] A Conrad student informed me in Scotland that Africa is merely a setting for the disintegration of the mind of Mr. Kurtz.

Which is partly the point. Africa as setting and backdrop which eliminates the African as human factor. Africa as a metaphysical battlefield devoid of all recognizable humanity, into which the wandering European enters at his peril. Can nobody see the preposterous and perverse arrogance in thus reducing Africa to the role of props for the break up of one petty European mind? But that is not even the point. The real question is the dehumanization of Africa and Africans which this age-long attitude has fostered and continues to foster in the world. And the question is whether a novel which celebrates this dehumanization, which depersonalizes a portion of the human race, can be called a great work of art. My answer is: No, it cannot.[11] I do not doubt Conrad's

79

great talents. Even *Heart of Darkness* has its memorably good passages and moments:

The reaches opened before us and closed behind, as if the forest had stepped leisurely across the water to bar the way for our return.

Its exploration of the minds of the European characters is often penetrating and full of insight. But all that has been more than fully discussed in the last fifty years. His obvious racism has, however, not been addressed. And it is high time it was.

Notes

4. "(and persons)" [1977]. The next two paragraphs (from "Fine fellows" to "a great comfort to look at") were added in 1988.

5. "great attention" [1977].

6. "a little imitation of Conrad" [1977].

7. Sentence added in 1988.

8. Quarantine barrier (French). [Editor]

9. "bloody" [1977].

10. The last clause (beginning "that the point of . . .") was added in 1988.

11. The rest of this paragraph was added in 1988, replacing the original version: "I would not call that man an artist, for example, who composes an eloquent instigation to one people to fall upon another and destroy them. No matter how striking his imagery or how beautiful his cadences fall, such a man is no more a great artist than another may be called a priest who reads the mass backwards or a physician who poisons his patents. All those men in Nazi Germany who lent their talent to the service of virulent racism whether in science, philosophy or the arts have generally and rightly been condemned for their perversions. The time is long overdue for taking a hard look at the work of creative artists who apply their talents, alas often considerable as in the case of Conrad, to set people against people. This, I take it, is what Yevtushenko is after when he tells us that a poet cannot be a slave trader at the same time, and gives the striking example of Arthur Rimbaud, who was fortunately honest enough to give up any pretenses to poetry when he opted for slave trading. For poetry surely can only be on the side of man's deliverance and not his enslavement; for the brotherhood and unity of all mankind and against the doctrines of Hitler's master races or Conrad's 'rudimentary souls.'"

Of the many mythic feminine figures in Conrad's novels and stories, one in particular has elicited fervent reactions: Kurtz's "small sketch in oils," in *Heart of Darkness*, representing a woman, draped and blindfolded, carrying a lighted torch" (46). As Marlow tells the men aboard the *Nellie*, "The background was somber—almost black. The movement of the woman was stately, and the effect of the torchlight on the face was sinister" (46–7). The figure in the painting recalls personifications of Liberty and Justice, who are associated with the amazonian ideal. Yet with the paired attributes of torch and blindfold this woman appears both potent and disturbingly powerless. Although Marlow mentions the painting only once in his embedded narrative, critics have been drawn to its paradoxical imagery as perhaps to few other word portraits in Conrad's writings. In their efforts to trace the painting's symbolic resonances, critics variously have seen the blindfolded, torch-bearing figure as a symbol for Kurtz (Karl 132, Sexton 388, DeKoven 113), for Europe "blinded by the light of her civilization" (Shaffer 2), or even for all "mankind, groping blindly through the darkness of his existence" (Dowden 158).

These readings hold in common a tendency to naturalize the figure in the painting. However, as Marina Warner explains, "a symbolized female presence both gives and takes value and meaning in relation to actual women" (xx). To see the painting's polysemous imagery in terms of a commentary on Kurtz's psychology, on Western imperialist ideology, or, most broadly of all, on the general "despair" of the human condition, is to elide attention to its presentation of a *female* figure. Jeremy Hawthorn, in a notable exception, links "Kurtz's portrait of the blindfolded female" to the European women characters in *Heart of Darkness* (183), but in a more subtle act of displacement he adds that these female characters are themselves icons who "serve a larger representative function, portraying that idealism which the western imperialist powers use as apology for their exploitation" (184). As he says, "the picture helps to support the argument that the novella associates the isolation of European women with the isolation of idealism from that which it is being used to underwrite" (190).[1] Yet not European women alone are associated with the painting's mythic figure (whose race has always been assumed by critics, but is never actually identified in the text).[2] Although Marlow allies the Intended with the figure in the painting, describing her paradigmatically raised arms as she stands surrounded by "an unearthly glow" (121), Marlow also recalls the upstretched arms and amazonian "helmeted head" of Kurtz's African mistress (108), and, in a direct echo of his description of the painting, declares that "there was something *ominous* and *stately* in her deliberate progress" along a lighted embankment by the Congo river (99, emphasis added).

Indeed, many of Conrad's female characters are to some degree implicated in the imagery of this painting, or the image of a blinded, light-bearing woman also appears in *Lord Jim, The Rescue*, and "The Return." . . .

By force of repetition, Conrad implies that, whether as essence or as social mandate, the relation between blindness and light is somehow bound up with women and femininity. No comparable image in Conrad's writings directly associates men with synchronous blindness and light-bearing. Although indirect associations abound, the effect is always to feminize male characters, who become at least momentarily, aligned with women. For example, in *Heart of Darkness* Marlow's aunt suggests that he is "something like an emissary of light" (28), but later in the narrative, Marlow compares himself to "a blindfolded man set to driving a van down a bad road" (60).[3] In this moment, Marlow is aligned with the Intended, for he is as "out of it" as she is (80). In other words, the gender of the figure in the painting from *Heart of Darkness* is neither casual nor incidental to its meaning; it maintains a significance that extends beyond an understanding of any one particular Conradian character or text, and certainly extends beyond how European women in Conrad's writings are isolated and exploited by imperialism. . . . Does the figure of a light-bearing

82

woman who cannot see by the light she casts prescribe woman's passivity and subjection? Does the figure take on the attributes of Liberty and Justice to underwrite an ideal of venerable feminine virtue? Or does the contrast between torch and blindfold on the allegorical body of woman escape traditional, masculine constructions of feminine lack (and impossible virtue) by making manifest the paradox in these mutually exclusive alternatives? . . .

Conrad's own attitudes toward femininity cannot be located in any one character's response, for in continually refiguring the image Conrad demands that we interpret it in a broader context, from various points of view across and within these tales. To understand his coded imagery, we must also account for the complex iconographic history that Conrad invokes with his representations of blinded torchbearers. Finally, this imagery demands to be interpreted in psychoanalytic terms, or it is linked to the fetish, which is a symbol of castrated, feminine power that empowers the male.

Notes

1. Marianne DeKoven notes that "what is most important about this painting is the way it connects Kurtz, in our crucial first impression, with both the power and the danger of the feminine" (113). DeKoven acknowledges that the painted image is "feminine," but her primary interest lies in what this image reveals not about women, but about its painter, Kurtz. She also makes the problematic assumption that there is something inherently dangerous about femininity. If femininity is a constructed psychic position applicable to Kurtz and other men as well as to women, then one must always keep in mind that this construction involves both transference and projection. In other words, one should always ask: dangerous to whom? Marlow thinks there is something "sinister" about the painting, but this is a projection on his part. As I will show, DeKoven takes for granted that which the novel subtly exposes as specious.

Hawthorn's argument, in contrast, is closest to my own. He links "Kurtz's portrait of the blindfolded female" to the European women characters in *Heart of Darkness* (183), and, ultimately, to the domestic oppression of the female sex during the heyday of European Imperialism (191). I will argue, however, that the "idealism critique" in the novel is no more and no less than the imaginary ideal of an absolute sexual difference.

83

2. Ruth Nadelhaft provides the exception, or she argues that the woman in the painting is in fact a black woman possibly inspired by Baudelaire's references to "*la negresse*" in his poem "Le Cygne." Nadelhaft writes: "That black woman might well be the subject of painting, in *Heart of Darkness*, a black woman 'draped and blindfolded, carrying a lighted torch'" [*sic*] (47). It seems to me, however, that she confuses the painting's background with the woman herself and that therefore her argument is somewhat forced; the text does not resolve the issue of the woman's race.

3. In *Heart of Darkness*, Marlow's aunt is an interesting example of woman's dual capacity for potency and powerlessness, for she is Marlow's connection to the hegemony that runs the exploitation in Africa. Her covert political influence, exerted from "a room that most soothingly looked just as you would expect a lady's drawing-room to look," is used in blind support of the "rot let loose in print and talk just about that time" (28). Isolated in her lady's drawing-room," she believes herself when she talks to Marlow about "weaning those ignorant millions from their horrid ways" (29). Since her "influential acquaintances" strike awe in Company employees, it is hard to think of her as exploited (47); yet she is utterly oblivious to the possibility that, as Marlow remarks, "the Company was run for profit" (28), and that its African ventures are little more than "robbery with violence, aggravated murder on a great scale" (20).

Works Cited

Conrad, Joseph. *Almayer's Folly*. Harmondsworth: Penguin, 1976.
———. *Heart of Darkness*. Harmondsworth: Penguin 1995.
DeKoven, Marianne. *Rich and Strange: Gender, History Modernism*. Princeton: Princeton University Press, 1991.
Dowden, Wilfred S. "The Light and Dark Lie." Conrad's *Heart of Darkness and the Critics*. Ed. Bruce Harkness. Belmont, CA: Wadsworth, 1960, 158–60.
Hawthorn, Jeremy. *Joseph Conrad: Narrative Technique and Ideological Commitment*. London: Edward Arnold Press, 1990.
Karl, Frederick, and Laurence Davies (eds.). *The Collected Letters of Joseph Conrad*. vols. to date. Cambridge: Cambridge University Press, 1983–.
Karl, Frederick. "Introduction to the *Danse Macabre*: Conrad's *Heart of Darkness*." *Heart of Darkness: A Case Study in Contemporary Criticism*. Ed. Ross C. Murfin. New York: St. Martin's Press, 1989, 123–36.
Sexton, Mark S. "Kurtz's Sketch in Oils: Its Significance to *Heart of Darkness*." *Studies in Short Fiction* 24:4 (Fall 1987): 387–92.
Shaffer, Brian W. *The Blinding Torch: Modern British Fiction and the Discourse of Civilization*. Amherst: University of Massachusetts Press, 1993.

Warner, Marina. *Monuments and Maidens: The Allegory of the Female Form.* New York: Athenaeum, 1985.

CEDRIC T. WATTS ON CRITICAL INTERPRETATION

Conrad's 'Heart of Darkness' is a rich, vivid, layered, paradoxical, and problematic novella or long tale; a mixture of oblique autobiography, traveller's yarn, adventure story, psychological odyssey, political satire, symbolic prose-poem, black comedy, spiritual melodrama, and sceptical meditation. It has proved to be 'ahead of its times': an exceptionally proleptic text. First published in 1899 as a serial in *Blackwood's Edinburgh Magazine*, it became extensively influential during subsequent decades, and reached a zenith of critical acclaim in the period 1950–75. During the final quarter of the twentieth century, however, while its influence became even more pervasive, the tale was vigorously assailed on political grounds by various feminist critics and by some left-wing and Third World commentators.[1]. . .

In a 1975 lecture, the distinguished Nigerian novelist, Chinua Achebe, declared that Conrad was 'a bloody racist' ('An Image of Africa', p. 788). Achebe asserted that 'Heart of Darkness' depicts Africa as 'a place of negations . . . in comparison with which Europe's own state of spiritual grace will be manifest' (p. 783). The Africans are dehumanized and degraded, seen as grotesques or as a howling mob. They are denied speech, or are granted speech only to condemn themselves out of their own mouths. We see 'Africa as setting and backdrop which eliminates the African as human factor. Africa as a metaphysical battlefield devoid of all recognizable humanity, into which the wandering European enters at his peril' (p. 788). The result, he says, is 'an offensive and totally deplorable book' that promotes racial intolerance and is therefore to be condemned.

Achebe's lecture had a powerful impact, and its text was repeatedly reprinted and widely discussed. 'Heart of Darkness', which had seemed to be bold and astute in its attacks on imperialism, was now revealed as a work that, in the opinion

85

of a leading African writer, was actually pro-imperialist in its endorsement of racial prejudice. The next onslaught came from feminist critics and had a similar basis. While Achebe had seen the Africans as marginalized and demeaningly stereotyped, various feminist critics felt that the tale similarly belittled women. Nina Pelikan Straus, Bette London, Johanna M. Smith, and Elaine Showalter were among those who claimed that 'Heart of Darkness' was not only imperialist but also 'sexist'. . . .

In short, a text that had once appeared to be 'ahead of its times', a nineteenth-century tale that anticipated twentieth-century cultural developments and epitomized twentieth-century concerns, now seemed to be dated—outstripped by recent advances. A text that had so often been praised for its political radicalism now looked politically reactionary. The problems raised by the controversy over the merits of 'Heart of Darkness' were now problems not merely about the reading of details but also about the very basis of evaluation of literary texts, about the relationship between literary appreciation and moral/political judgement. . . .

A standard procedure, illustrated by Achebe and Straus, is to judge the tale according to whether its inferred political outlook tallies with that of the critic: to the extent that the critic's views are reflected, the tale is commended; to the extent that they are not, the tale is condemned. This procedure is familiar but odd. It assumes the general validity of the critic's outlook; but different people have different outlooks. Moreover, the critic's outlook may not remain constant, but may be modified by experience, including encounters with literary works. In this respect, 'Heart of Darkness' seems to ambush its adversaries. Marlow has been changed by his experience of Africa, and is still being changed. One of the subtlest features of the text is the dramatization of his uncertainties, of his tentativeness, of his groping for affirmations that his own narrative subsequently questions. Through Marlow, this liminal and protean novella renders the process of teaching and learning, and of negotiating alternative viewpoints. To take an obvious example: he offers conflicting interpretations of Kurtz's cry, 'The horror! The horror!'. Perhaps they refer to Kurtz's corruption, perhaps to the horror of a senseless universe. But there may be another meaning: no final resolution is offered. Marlow addresses a group of friends on a vessel. They may not share his views; and, indeed, they voice dissent—'Try to be civil'; 'Absurd'. A commentator who declares Conrad 'racist' or 'sexist' may be imposing on Conrad readily available stereotypes, but, at its best, the tale questions the process of imposing stereotypes. Such phrases as 'weaning those ignorant millions', 'enemies, criminals, workers . . . rebels', 'unsound method' or 'leader of an extreme party' are invested with sardonic irony. In addition, a political commentator on the text may seem imperialistic in seeking to incorporate literary terrain within the territory of his or her own personal value-system. If we abolished all those past texts that, to our fallible understandings, failed to endorse present values or prejudices, few works would survive. A literary work may have a diversity of political implications and consequences, but it is not a political manifesto. It is an imaginative work that offers a voluntary and hypothetical experience. Its linguistic texture may be progressive when its readily paraphrasable content may not. All its implications remain within the invisible quotation marks of the fictional. In other works, the same author could, of course, deploy quite different materials with contrasting implications. In 'Heart of Darkness', Marlow says that women are out of touch with truth; but in *Chance*, he says that women see 'the whole truth', whereas men live in a 'fool's paradise' (p. 144). Meanwhile, in 1910, Conrad signed a formal letter to the Prime Minister, Herbert Asquith, advocating votes for women (*Letters*, IV, p. 327).[18] Awareness of Conrad's complexity may entail recognition of a currently widespread critical habit: the reductive falsification of the past in an attempt to vindicate the political gestures of the present. 'Heart of Darkness' reminds us that this habit resembles an earlier one: the adoption of a demeaning attitude to colonized people in the attempt to vindicate the exploitative actions of the colonizer. The 'pilgrims' in the tale have fathered some of the pundits of today.

We read fiction for pleasures of diverse kinds; and Conrad earned his living as an entertainer, not as a writer of religious or political tracts. The pleasures generated by 'Heart of Darkness' have many sources. They lie in part in its evocative vividness, its modes of suspense, its originality, and its power to provoke thought. Paraphrase is a necessary critical tool, but paraphrase is never an equivalent of the original, whose vitality lies in its combination of particular and general, of rational and emotional. A political scansion of the work is not the only mode of scansion, nor is it necessarily the most illuminating. Literary criticism has an identity distinct from political advocacy, just as creative writing is distinct from political non-fiction. As the text moves through time, the changing historical and cultural circumstances will variously increase and reduce its cogency. Texts may thus apparently die for a period and then regain their vitality. Shakespeare's *King Lear* vanished from the stage for about 150 years, and audiences seeing *King Lear* in the eighteenth century saw Nahum Tate's play, not Shakespeare's. May Sinclair's fine novel, *Life and Death of Harriett Frean* (1922), was neglected for decades until Virago Press republished it. The reputation of 'Heart of Darkness' is now a matter of controversy, and its standing may decline; but its complexity guarantees that it will prove fruitful to many readers for a long time yet. . . .

One of the features that made it outstanding among texts of the 1890s was its recognition of the disparities between the realities of experience and the inadequacies of conventional interpretations of it. The tale repeatedly implies an irreducible excess that eludes summary. It may thus warn commentators that they, confined to the limited discourse of rational non-fictional prose, are likely to be outdistanced by the multiple resources of the fictional text. The anonymous narrator speaks with romantic eloquence of all the great men who have sailed forth on the Thames, but Marlow interjects 'And this also . . . has been one of the dark places of the earth', and proceeds to remind him that Britain would once have seemed as savage a wilderness to Roman colonizers as Africa now seems to Europeans. This is a rebuke to empire-builders and to believers in the durability of civilization;

it invokes a humiliating chronological perspective; and it may jolt the reader into circumspection. Reflections on this passage might induce caution in any commentator who initially fails to relate 'Heart of Darkness' fairly to the time of its writing, or who assumes the superiority of a present-day viewpoint that is itself a product of the times: 'We live in the flicker'. As 'Heart of Darkness' repeatedly implies, a value judgement cannot, in logic, be deduced from a statement of fact. The narrative is partly about the struggle to maintain a humane morality when that morality no longer seems to bear guaranteed validity. In this respect, 'Heart of Darkness' remains cogent and may teach circumspection to its critics. The tale has sombre implications, and so has the story of its reception over the years, but the eloquence, virtuosity, and intensity with which 'Heart of Darkness' addressed its era were exemplary, and seem likely to ensure its longevity.

Notes

1. This novella's critical fortunes may be traced in Sherry, ed., *Conrad: The Critical Heritage*, Harkness, ed., *Conrad's 'Heart of Darkness' and the Critics*, Murfin, ed., *Joseph Conrad: 'Heart of Darkness': A Case Study in Contemporary Criticism*, Bloom, ed., *Joseph Conrad's 'Heart of Darkness'*, Carabine, ed., *Joseph Conrad: Critical Assessments*, Kimbrough's Norton volumes of 1963, 1971, and 1988, and Burden, *'Heart of Darkness': An Introduction to the Variety of Criticism*. Fothergill's *Heart of Darkness* provides a useful introductory summary.

18. See also Davies, 'Conrad, *Chance*, and women readers'.

Works Cited

Achebe, Chinua. 'An image of Africa: racism in Conrad's "Heart of Darkness"'. *Massachusetts Review* 17.4 (1977), 782–94. Reprinted (revised) in Kimbrough, ed., *Joseph Conrad's 'Heart of Darkness'*, pp. 251–62.

Baudelaire, Charles. *Les Fleurs du mal*. 1857. Paris: Aux quais de Paris, 1957.

Bloom, Harold, ed. *Joseph Conrad's 'Heart of Darkness'*. New York: Chelsea House, 1987.

Burden, Robert. *'Heart of Darkness': An Introduction to the Variety of Criticism*. London: Macmillan, 1991.

Carabine, Keith, ed. *Joseph Conrad: Critical Assessments*. 4 vols. Robertsbridge: Helm Information, 1992.

Conrad, Joseph. *Chance*. 1914. Ed. Martin Ray. Oxford: Oxford University Press, 1988.

———. *'Heart of Darkness' and Other Tales*. Ed. Cedric Watts. Oxford: Oxford University Press, 1990.

———. 'A Familiar Preface'. *'The Mirror of the Sea' and 'A Personal Record'*. 1906 and 1912. Ed. Zdzislaw Najder. Oxford: Oxford University Press, 1988, pp. xi–xxi.

———. 'Geography and some explorers'. 1924. *Last Essays*. Ed. Richard Curie. London: Dent, 1926. Reprinted 1955, pp. 1–22.

Cox, C. B. Introduction. *Youth: A Narrative/Heart of Darkness/The End of the Tether*. London: Dent; Vermont: Tuttle, 1974.

Davies, Laurence. 'Conrad, *Chance*, and women readers'. *The Conradian* 17.1 (1993), 75–88.

Eagleton, Terry. *Criticism and Ideology: A Study in Marxist Literary Theory*. London: Verso, 1976.

Eliot, T. S. *The Waste Land: A Facsimile and Transcript of the Original Drafts including the Annotations of Ezra Pound*. Ed. Valerie Eliot. London: Faber & Faber, 1971.

———. *Selected Essays*. London: Faber & Faber, 1951.

———. '*Ulysses*, order and myth'. *The Dial* 75 (1923), 480–3.

Evans, Robert O. 'Conrad's underworld'. *Modern Fiction Studies* 2.2 (1956), 56–92.

Feder, Lillian. 'Marlow's descent into hell'. *Nineteenth Century Fiction* 9.4 (1955), 280–92.

Fothergill, Anthony. *Heart of Darkness*. Milton Keynes: Open University Press, 1989.

Harkness, Bruce, ed. *Conrad's 'Heart of Darkness' and the Critics*. Belmont, CA: Wadsworth, 1960.

Harris, Wilson. 'The frontier on which "Heart of Darkness" stands'. *Research on African Literatures* 12 (1981), 86–92. Reprinted Kimbrough, ed., *Joseph Conrad's 'Heart of Darkness'*, pp. 262–8.

Hawkins, Hunt. 'Conrad's critique of imperialism'. *PMLA* 94 (1979), 286–99.

Jung, C. B. *Modern Man in Search of a Soul*. London: Routledge & Kegan Paul, 1933. Reprinted 1966.

Kimbrough, Robert, ed. *Joseph Conrad's 'Heart of Darkness'*. 3rd edn. New York: Norton, 1988.

Leavis, F. R. *The Great Tradition: George Eliot, Henry James, Joseph Conrad*. London: Chatto & Windus; New York: G. W. Stewart, 1948. Reprinted Harmondsworth: Penguin Books, 1962.

London, Bette. *The Appropriated Voice: Narrative Authority in Conrad, Forster, and Woolf*. Ann Arbor: University of Michigan Press, 1990.

Murfin, Ross C., ed. *Joseph Conrad: 'Heart of Darkness': A Case Study in Contemporary Criticism*. New York: Bedford Books of St Martin's Press, 1989.

Najder, Zdzislaw. *Joseph Conrad: A Chronicle*. Tr. Halina Carroll-Najder. New Brunswick, NJ: Rutgers University Press; Cambridge: Cambridge University Press, 1983.

Sarvan, C. P. 'Racism and the *Heart of Darkness*'. *International Fiction Review* 7 (1980), 6–10. Reprinted Kimbrough, ed., *Joseph Conrad's 'Heart of Darkness'*, pp. 280–5.

Sherry, Norman. *Conrad's Western World*. Cambridge: Cambridge University Press, 1971.

———, ed. *Conrad: The Critical Heritage*. London: Routledge & Kegan Paul, 1973.

Showalter, Elaine. *Sexual Anarchy*. London: Bloomsbury, 1991.

Smith, Johanna M. '"Too beautiful altogether": patriarchal ideology in "Heart of Darkness"'. In *Joseph Conrad: 'Heart of Darkness': A Case Study in Contemporary Criticism*. Ed. Ross C. Murfin. New York: Bedford Books of St Martin's Press, 1989, pp. 179–95.

Steiner, George. *The Portage to San Cristobal of A. H.* London: Faber & Faber, 1981.

Stone, Robert. *Dog Soldiers*. London: Secker & Warburg, 1975. Reprinted London: Pan Books, 1988.

Straus, Nina Pelikan. 'The exclusion of the Intended from secret sharing in Conrad's "Heart of Darkness"'. *Novel* 20.2 (1987), 123–37.

Thiong'o, Ngugi Wa. *A Grain of Wheat*. London: Heinemann, 1967. Reset 1975.

Watt, Ian. *Conrad in the Nineteenth Century*. Berkeley: University of California Press, 1979; London: Chatto & Windus, 1980.

Watts, Cedric. *Conrad's 'Heart of Darkness': A Critical and Contextual Discussion*. Milan: Mursia, 1977.

———. *The Deceptive Text: An Introduction to Covert Plots*. Brighton: Harvester; Totowa, NJ: Barnes & Noble, 1984.

———. *A Preface to Conrad*. 2nd edn. London: Longman, 1993.

MARVIN MUDRICK ON THE ORIGINALITY OF CONRAD

Conrad offers himself from the first as a dogged innovator of fictional techniques, like his own Kurtz one of the first thorough explorers of a rather dark continent; and it is tempting to read him for the sophisticated pleasure one takes in recognizing novel and schematizable, if not necessarily expressive, method. . . .

Length is usually, indeed, no advantage to Conrad. Albert Guerard has asserted that "Conrad's long stories and short novels are far more experimental and more 'modern' than his full-length novels"[2]; and, though it is an assertion that requires reservations, it points to the comparative economy and tact of Conrad's method in pieces like *Typhoon* and *The Nigger of the "Narcissus,"* to the unfailing grim power of Part First of *Under Western Eyes* (before the novel falls apart in a compulsion to extend itself beyond its normal novella length), as well as to the inert and wilful complications characteristic of such larger works as *Chance, Lord Jim, Victory, Nostromo,* and *The Secret Agent.* Everything Conrad wrote recalls everything else he wrote, in a pervasive melancholy of outlook, a persistency of theme ("the plight of the man on whom life closes down inexorably, divesting him of the supports and illusory protection of friendship. social privilege or love"[3]) and a conscientious manipulation of innovational method; yet what marks Conrad as not a mere experimentalist or entertainer but a genuine innovator occurs only sporadically in his full-length novels, with discretion and sustained impulse only in several long stories or short novels: in *The Nigger of the "Narcissus,"* in *Typhoon,* in Part First of *Under Western Eyes* and—with most impressive rich immediacy—in *Heart of Darkness.*

Conrad's innovation—or, in any case the fictional technique that he exploited with unprecedented thoroughness—is the double plot: neither allegory (where surface is something teasing to be got through), nor catch-all symbolism (where every knowing particular signifies some universal or other), but a developing order of actions so lucidly symbolic of a developing state of spirit—from moment to moment so morally identifiable—as to suggest the conditions of allegory without forfeiting or even subordinating the realistic "superficial" claim of the actions and their actors.

Heart of Darkness—at least until we reach Kurtz and the end of the journey—is a remarkable instance of such order: details intensely present, evocatively characteristic of the situations in which they happen, and prefiguring from moment to moment an unevadable moral reality. . . .

The work defines and embodies itself in its reluctant functionaries, starched accountant as well as dying natives; it has its particular counter-sign and gleaming talisman ("'The word "ivory" rang in the air, was whispered, was sighed. You would think they were praying to it. A taint of imbecile rapacity blew through it all, like a whiff from some corpse'"); in its tangible promise of easy gratifications, it indifferently victimizes both the unwilling natives and their incompetent overseers, it prescribes the tableau of cruelty in the grove of death, it provides its own corresponding niche for every stage of opportunism from the novice exploiter (weight 224 pounds) who keeps fainting, to the manager of the Central Station, the man with the single talent and the essential defect—

"He was obeyed, yet he inspired neither love nor fear, nor even respect. He inspired uneasiness. That was it! Uneasiness. Not a definite mistrust—just uneasiness—nothing more. You have no idea how effective such a .. a ... faculty can be. ... Once when various tropical diseases had laid low almost every 'agent' in the station, he was heard to say, 'Men who come out here should have no entrails.'"

The general blight and demoralization are inextricable, they do not detach themselves for scrutiny, from the developing order of actions that intensely brings them to mind; they have no independent symbolic existence, nor do any other of the spreading abstractions and big ideas in the narrative. Even the journey into the heart of darkness—the more obvious broad symbolic provocations of which have given joy to so many literary amateurs—insofar as it has artistic (rather than merely psychoanalytic) force, is finely coincident with its network of details; its moral nature steadily reveals itself not in the rather predictable grand gestures of Conradian rhetoric ("'Going upriver was like going back to beginnings, when vegetation rioted and the big trees were kings'"), but in the unavoidable facts of suspense, strangeness, vigilance, danger, and fear: the difficulties of piloting the patched fragile steamer past hidden banks, snags, sunken stones upriver; the sudden "'glimpse of rush walls, of peaked grass roofs, a burst of yells, a whirl of black limbs, a mass of hands clapping, of feet stamping, of bodies swaying, of eyes rolling, under the droop of heavy and motionless foliage'"; the honest, "'unmistakably real'" book mysteriously discovered in the abandoned hut; the terrified savage tending the boiler, who "'squinted at the steam gauge with an evident effort of intrepidity'"; the arrows from nowhere; the death of the black helmsman ("'The man had rolled on his back and stared straight up at me; both his hands clutched that cane. It was the shaft of a spear that, either thrown or lunged through the opening, had caught him in the side just below the ribs; the blade had gone in out of sight, after making a frightful gash; my shoes were full; a pool of blood lay very still, gleaming dark-red under the wheel; his eyes shone with an amazing luster'"); and, most shocking of all in its evocation of mind at an intolerable extremity, the climactic farcical detail of Marlow's panic to get rid of his shoes and socks overflowing with a dead man's blood—

> "To tell you the truth, I was morbidly anxious to change my shoes and socks. 'He is dead,' murmured the fellow, immensely impressed. 'No doubt about it,' said I, tugging like mad at the shoelaces."

When Conrad is called, with a clear confidence that the judgment is general and will not be challenged "perhaps the finest prose stylist"[4] among the English novelists, it is doubtless such passages as these that the critic has in mind. One wonders, then, what the critic makes of such equally representative Conradian passages as the following:

> "It was the stillness of an implacable force brooding over an inscrutable intention."

> "I tried to break the spell—the heavy, mute spell of the wilderness—that seemed to draw him to its pitiless breast

by the awakening of forgotten and brutal instincts, by the memory of gratified and monstrous passions."

"I heard a light sigh and then my heart stood still, stopped dead short by an exulting and terrible cry, by the cry of inconceivable triumph and of unspeakable pain. 'I knew it—I was sure!' . . . She knew. She was sure."

Qualifying his account of Conrad as one of the four masters of English fiction, Dr. Leavis makes the definitive comment on this sort of thing: "Conrad must here stand convicted of borrowing the arts of the magazine-writer (who has borrowed his, shall we say, from Kipling and Poe) in order to impose on his readers and on himself, for thrilled response, a significance that is merely an emotional insistence on the presence of what he can't produce. The insistence betrays the absence, the willed 'intensity', the nullity. He is intent on making a virtue out of not knowing what he means."[5]

Qualification, however, is not enough. Conrad's lapses of this sort are not rare or incidental, they do not merely weaken his master style but schismatically parallel it in a style of their own. . . .

Conrad's symbolism, and his moral imagination, are, after all, as un-allegorical as possible. When they function and have effect they are severely realistic: they nourish themselves on voices heard and solid objects seen and touched in the natural world, they contract into rhetoric as soon as the voices and objects begin to appear less than independently present; when Conrad is not describing, with direct sensuous impact, a developing sequence of distinct actions, he is liable to drift into the mooning or glooming that for some critics passes as Conrad's "philosophy" and for others as his style in its full tropical luxuriance.

Moreover, to assume, as Dr. Leavis seems to assume, that all symbolism works *only* as it is anchored to a record of immediate sensations, that it must totally coincide with "the concrete presentment of incident, setting and image," is to transform Conrad's limitation (and gift) into a condition of fiction. To compare Conrad's symbolic method, his two-ply plot, with the methods of, say, Dostoevsky and Kafka is to become aware of radically different possibilities: on the one hand, Conrad's realistic mode, on the other, moral imaginations not necessarily anchored to objects and places, symbolic means capable of producing, for example, those vibrations of clairvoyant hallucination in Dostoevsky, and of meaningful enigma in Kafka, which move through and beyond immediate sensations into a world of moral meanings almost as independent as, and far more densely populated than, the other side of the mirror of traditional allegory. Of such effects, beyond the capacities of even the most evocative realism, Conrad is innocent; yet when, in *Heart of Darkness*, he approaches the center of a difficult moral situation (desperately more troublesome than the simple choices permitted the characters in *Typhoon*), when facts and details begin to appear inadequate as figurations of the moral problem, it is just such effects that he is at length driven to attempt. . . .

It is in fact one of those mixed structures whose partial success (not so neatly separable as, for example, Part First of *Under Western Eyes*), is so profound, so unprecedented, and so strikingly irreplaceable as to survive a proportion and gravity of failure that would sink forever any other work.

It is one of the great originals of literature. After *Heart of Darkness* the craftsman in fiction could never again be unaware of the moral resources inherent in every recorded sensation, or insensitive to the need of making the most precise record possible of every sensation: what now appears an immemorial cliché of the craft of fiction has a date as recent as the turn of the century. If Conrad was never quite equal to his own originality, he was at least the first to designate it as a new province of possibilities for the novelist and, in *Heart of Darkness*, the first to suggest, by large and compelling partial proof, the intensity of moral illumination that a devoted attention to its demands might generate. The suggestion was an historical event: for good and bad novelists alike, irreversible. After *Heart of Darkness*, the recorded moment—the word—was irrecoverably symbol.

Notes

2. Conrad, *Heart of Darkness* and *The Secret Sharer*, introd. Albert Guerard (New York: Signet, 1950), p. 8.

3. Zabel, *The Portable Conrad*, p. 26.

4. Conrad, *Heart of Darkness* and *The Secret Sharer*, p. 7.

5. F. R. Leavis, *The Great Tradition* (New York: Anchor, 1954), p. 219.

GENE M. MOORE ON CONRAD'S INFLUENCE

If it is true, as Conrad once wrote, that 'A man's real life is that accorded to him in the thoughts of other men' (*UWE*, p. 14), then the real life of Joseph Conrad is manifest throughout modern and contemporary literature, and has become a living part of our cultural self-awareness. His works have been translated into more than forty languages, from Albanian and Yiddish to Korean and Swahili. Conrad is one of the defining founders of literary Modernism, and his influence has been acknowledged by writers as different from him, and from each other, as André Gide, Ralph Ellison, Graham Greene, Jorge Luis Borges, V. S. Naipaul, William S. Burroughs, and Italo Calvino, to name only a few. Some of his works have been taken as models for the development of new literary genres. *The Secret Agent* and *Under Western Eyes* were among the first studies of spies who cannot come in from the cold, *Nostromo* is the first panoramic epic of South American colonialism, and 'Heart of Darkness' is frequently invoked as a cultural token signifying the 'horror' at the heart of modern Western civilization. The life and works of Conrad have inspired films, journeys, sculptures, comic books, Conrad societies and journals, and well over one thousand academic books and articles.

Why have Conrad's works had such a profound influence on the way we perceive and define the modern condition? The answer has something to do with the sense in which Conrad is a figure of the crossroads, determined to portray and explore the conflicting loyalties and multiple identities of those who, like him, have been denied their cultural birthright.

Conrad writes with the passionate irony of an exile, from the necessarily false position of a cultural colonist who speaks, in a language not quite his own, for both the dispossessed and their dispossessors. . . .

ANXIETIES OF INFLUENCE

Conrad had a greater personal experience of 'Third World' populations than most writers of his time, and the protagonists of his first two novels, Kaspar Almayer and Peter Willems, are memorable examples of the moral degeneracy of colonialism founded on racial prejudice. Almayer is devastated when his daughter Nina rejects his Eurocentric ambitions in favour of a native prince, while Aïssa in *An Outcast of the Islands* castigates Willems's homeland as 'A land of lies and of evil from which nothing but misfortune ever comes to us—who are not white' (*OI*, p. 144). It is therefore not surprising that Conrad's influence has been deeply felt by writers who have sought to chronicle the human history of colonies and the struggles of those seeking a *modus vivendi* between the rights and claims of native traditions and the access to a larger world available through Western technologies and means of communication. For some, like Achebe, Conrad remains hopelessly Anglophile and racist, while others have found in his works a subtle and complex mixture of cultural awareness with imperialist blindness: thus, although writers like V. S. Naipaul and Edward Said greatly admire Conrad's achievement, Naipaul has characterized *Lord Jim* as an 'imperialist' novel with a 'racial straggler' for a hero, and Said has described a similar imperialist bias in *Nostromo*.

Conrad has had a profound influence on African novelists writing in English. Jacqueline Bardolphe has claimed that in the work of the Kenyan novelist Ngugi Wa Thiong'o, 'Conrad's work is not an "influence" but a fundamental intertext . . . in such a determining way that the two major novels [*A Grain of Wheat* (1967) and *Petals of Blood* (1977)] are "parodies" in the full sense that they provide readings of Conrad' ('Ngugi Wa Thiong'o's *A Grain of Wheat* and *Petals of Blood*', p. 37). In *Mawsim al-hedjra ilâ al-shimâl* (*Season of Migration to the North*,

1969), by the Sudanese writer Tayyib Sâlih, the hero reverses the direction of Marlow's voyage in 'Heart of Darkness'.[7]

V. S. Naipaul has described his encounters with Conrad in an eloquent essay entitled 'Conrad's Darkness', but his major fictional tribute to Conrad's legacy remains *A Bend in the River* (1979), which retells the story of 'Heart of Darkness' from the 'other side', from the perspective of the Islamic and Hindu colonialism of the east coast of Africa. Naipaul's account of a young man who takes up shopkeeping in a village that had been Kurtz's Inner Station only seventy years earlier is filled with commentaries on the difficulty of maintaining a sense of cultural identity between the pressures of Western domination and the weight of a less hegemonic, but no less colonial tradition lacking sophisticated terms for self-justification. Thus, in passages like the following, Naipaul's narrator clarifies what Marlow may have meant when he asserted that the only justification for colonial exploitation lay in the 'idea' behind it:

> If it was Europe that gave us on the coast some idea of our history, it was Europe, I feel, that also introduced us to the lie. Those of us who had been in that part of Africa before the Europeans had never lied about ourselves. Not because we were more moral. We didn't lie because we never assessed ourselves and didn't think there was anything for us to lie about; we were people who simply did what we did. But the Europeans could do one thing and say something quite different; and they could act in this way because they had an idea of what they owed to their civilization. It was their great advantage over us. (*A Bend in the River*, pp. 16–17)

The ambiguities of what we 'owe' to our civilization, and the hypocrisies of what it demands of us in return, are among Conrad's abiding themes. Naipaul has also relived Conrad's struggle for recognition as an English novelist despite his foreign origins, and he has often, like Conrad, been confronted with misunderstanding and disapproval from both sides. Third World ideologues have criticized him for his dreary portrayals of the garbage and litter of the colonies and for his enigmatic desire to enact the life of an English gentleman, while Western critics find it difficult to accept him other than as a Third World writer whose aspirations to 'arrival' are dismissed as a presumptuous dereliction of his duty to his 'own' people. This situation closely resembles Conrad's struggles to gain acceptance as an English writer and not merely as a curious case of linguistic and cultural assimilation. If, as Romain Gary suggested, the English could never fully accept Conrad as 'one of us', others have been eager to reclaim him for Poland by arguing that the essence of his achievement can best be understood in terms of a guilt-ridden 'betrayal' of his cultural origins.

In terms of this cultural conflict, the writer whose personal situation most directly re-enacted the case of Conrad is Jerzy Kosinski, whose last book, *The Hermit of 69th Street* (1988), is an obsessive compendium of self-conscious witticisms, snippets of Talmudic or philosophical wisdom (complete with footnotes and references), parenthetical correctives to the printer, and recurring allusions to sexual encounters, psychoanalysis, yoga, and the Holocaust.[8] It also includes a great many references to Conrad. Like Conrad, Kosinski survived an oppressive regime to achieve fame as a stylist in an adopted language, and, like Conrad, he paid a heavy price for the transformation: where Conrad's cultural and personal neuroses expressed themselves in chronic gout, hypochondria, and a series of nervous breakdowns, Kosinski's childhood traumas took the more drastic form of paranoia and ultimately suicide. Kosinski's very name shares its initials with Józef Korzeniowski, and the name of his protagonist, Norbert Kosky, is virtually a phonic anagram of Conrad's original surname. . . .

THE LEGACY OF JOSEPH CONRAD

Why has Conrad's influence been so extensive and profound? What is it about the example of his life and the record of his works that modern writers and readers have found so appealing? Perhaps an answer lies in the rare combination of the remarkable range of his experience with the fathomless depths of his irony.

Conrad was one of the first Western writers to give voice to the claims and aspirations of non-Western peoples. His own lack of a national homeland led him to speak for a larger constituency, and the essential statelessness of his own condition is reflected in the wide variety of national types that people his fictions. The protagonists of his first two novels are Dutch colonials, Nostromo is a South American immigrant of Italian origin, Razumov is an uprooted Russian, and Heyst is of Swedish descent. Mr Verloc's background is obscurely continental, and 'all Europe' contributed to the making of Kurtz. In *Lord Jim*, the crew of the *Patna* offers a typical example of the many nationalities to be met in Conrad's works: the owner is Chinese, the skipper is 'a sort of renegade New South Wales German' (p. 14), the second engineer is Cockney English, the helmsmen are Malay, and the 'cargo' consists of 800 Muslim pilgrims. Although Conrad remained an ardent Anglophile, his work embodies a lifelong commitment to the recognition voiced in the 'Author's Note' to his first novel, that 'there is a bond between us and that humanity so far away' (*AF*, p. 3). He remained faithful to this bond, and as the world has grown smaller we have come to understand him as an early and powerful advocate of the essential oneness of humankind. Marlow claimed that Jim was 'one of us', but the 'us' in his phrase includes us all.

As an expatriate determined to earn his living as a writer in an acquired language, Conrad was locked in a constant and fundamental struggle with words. He could never achieve the confidence of a native speaker of English, and this want of a linguistic and cultural birthright found expression in the haunting ironies and ambiguities of his style. As T. E. Lawrence observed, 'all things end in a kind of hunger, a suggestion of something he can't say or do or think' (Garnett, ed., *Letters of T. E. Lawrence*, p. 302). Like the language teacher who narrates *Under Western Eyes*, Conrad knew only too well that 'Words . . . are the great foes of reality' (*UWE*, p. 3). Modern literature is the creation of linguistic exiles, but unlike Joyce or Nabokov, Conrad was never tempted to celebrate his extraterritoriality by means of puns or neologisms. Instead, the fundamental insecurity of his cultural identity is embedded in the tone of his narrative voice, which speaks towards an idea of home from a condition of radical and multiple otherness. In the opening chapter of Conrad's last novel, *Suspense*, Cosmo Latham encounters a stranger, a 'secret sharer' named Attilio, who tells him how he once abandoned his ship to join a hermit in the wilderness. After hearing the story, Cosmo asks him: 'You deserted from your ship simply because the tone of his voice appealed to your heart. Is that your meaning?' and Attilio replies, 'You have guessed it, signorino' (*Su*, p. 7). There is perhaps no better explanation for Conrad's enduring influence.

Notes

7. For a comparison of *Nostromo* with *Petals of Blood*, see Fincham, 'Orality, literacy, and community'. A brief survey of Conrad's influence on African writers is found in Nazareth, 'Conrad's descendants'. *Joseph Conrad: Third World Perspectives*, Hamner, ed., reprints a number of important essays and provides an annotated bibliography of materials on Conrad and the colonial world.

8. Kosinski's Kosky evidently found it impossible to read his own proofs, and the printers he so frequently taunted appear to have taken their revenge, since the volume contains a great many errata.

Works Cited

Achebe, Chinua. 'An image of Africa: racism in Conrad's "Heart of Darkness"'. *Massachusetts Review* 17.4 (1977), 782–94. Reprinted in Hamner, ed., pp. 119–29

Bardolphe, Jacqueline. 'Ngugi Wa Thiong'o's *A Grain of Wheat* and *Petals of Blood* as readings of Conrad's *Under Western Eyes* and *Victory*'. *The Conradian* 12.1 (1987), 32–49

Bloom, Harold. *The Anxiety of Influence*. Oxford: Oxford University Press, 1973

Borges, Jorge Luis. *Borges: A Reader*. Ed. Emir Rodriguez Monegal and Alastair Reid. New York: Dutton, 1981

———. *Doctor Brodie's Report*. Tr. Norman Thomas di Giovanni. New York: Dutton, 1972

Brebach, Raymond. *Joseph Conrad, Ford Madox Ford, and the Making of 'Romance'*. Ann Arbor: UMI Research Press, 1985

Burgin, Richard. *Conversations with Jorge Luis Borges*. 1969. New York: Avon, 1970

Carabine, Keith. 'Conrad and American literature: a review essay'. *The Conradian* 13.2 (1988), 207–19

Conrad, Joseph. *Almayer's Folly*. 1895. Ed. Floyd Eugene Eddleman and David Leon Higdon. Cambridge: Cambridge University Press, 1994

———. *Lord Jim*. 1900. Ed. John Batchelor. Oxford: Oxford University Press, 1983

———. *An Outcast of the Islands*. 1896. Ed. J. H. Stape and Hans van Marie. Oxford: Oxford University Press, 1992

———. *Suspense*. 1925. Ed. Richard Curie. London: Dent, 1954

———. *Under Western Eyes*. 1911. Ed. Jeremy Hawthorn. Oxford: Oxford University Press, 1983

Daleski, H. M. 'A Perfect Spy and a great tradition'. *Journal of Narrative Technique* 20.1 (1990), 56–64

Fincham, Gail. 'Orality, literacy, and community: Conrad's *Nostromo* and Ngugi's *Petals of Blood*'. *The Conradian* 17.1 (1992), 45–71

Ford, Ford Madox. *Joseph Conrad. A Personal Remembrance*. London: Duckworth, 1924

García Márquez, Gabriel. *Love in the Time of Cholera*. Tr. Edith Grossman. New York: Knopf, 1988

Garnett, David, ed. *The Letters of T. E. Lawrence*. London: Cape, 1938

Gary, Romain. *La Nuit sera calme*. Paris: Gallimard, 1974

Gillon, Adam. '*The Radiant Line*: a new Polish novel about Conrad'. *Conradiana* 17.2 (1985), 109–17

———. '*The Affair in Marseilles*: another Polish novel about Conrad' *Conradiana* 25.1 (1993), 53–67

Greene, Graham. *In Search of a Character*. 1961. Harmondsworth: Penguin Books, 1968

Hamner, Robert D., ed. *Joseph Conrad. Third World Perspectives*. Washington, DC: Three Continents Press, 1990

Hemingway, Ernest. 'Conrad, optimist and moralist'. 1924. Reprinted in *By-Line: Ernest Hemingway*. Ed. William White. New York: Bantam, 1968, pp. 114–15

Hervouet, Yves. *The French Face of Joseph Conrad*. Cambridge: Cambridge University Press, 1990

Huggan, Graham. 'Anxieties of influence: Conrad in the Caribbean'. *Commonwealth* 11.1 (1988), 1–12

Kirschner, Paul. *Conrad: The Psychologist as Artist*. Edinburgh: Oliver & Boyd, 1968

Kleiner, Elaine L. 'Joseph Conrad's forgotten role in the emergence of science fiction'. *Extrapolation* 15 (1973), 25–34

Knowles, Owen. 'Conrad, Anatole France, and the early French Romantic tradition: some influences'. *Conradiana* 11.1 (1979), 41–61

Lansbury, James. *Korzeniowski*. London: Serpent's Tail, 1992

Laube, Horst. *Zwischen den Flussen: Reisen zu Joseph Conrad*. Frankfurt: Syndikat, 1982

Long, Robert Emmet. '*The Great Gatsby* and the tradition of Joseph Conrad'. *Texas Studies in Literature and Language* 8 (1966), 257–76, 407–22

Lowry, Malcolm. 'Joseph Conrad'. *The Collected Poetry of Malcolm Lowry*. Ed. Kathleen Scherf. Vancouver: UBC Press, 1992, pp. 117–18

Ludwig, Richard M., ed. *Letters of Ford Madox Ford*. Princeton: Princeton University Press, 1965

Meriwether, James, B. and Michael Millgate, ed. *Lion in the Garden: Interviews with William Faulkner, 1926–1962*. Lincoln: University of Nebraska Press, 1968

Meyers, Jeffrey. 'Conrad's influence on modern writers'. *Twentieth Century Literature* 36.2 (1990), 186–206

Mizener, Arthur. *The Far Side of Paradise: A Biography of F. Scott Fitzgerald*. New York: Vintage, 1959

Morey, John Hope. 'Joseph Conrad and Ford Madox Ford: a study in collaboration'. Unpublished PhD thesis, Cornell University, 1960

Morf, Gustav. *The Polish Heritage of Joseph Conrad*. London: Sampson Low, Marston, 1930

Nabokov, Vladimir. *Strong Opinions*. London: Weidenfeld & Nicolson, 1973

Naipaul, V. S. *A Bend in the River*. 1979. New York: Vintage, 1980

———. 'Conrad's darkness'. 1974. In *The Return of Eva Perón*. New York: Vintage, 1981, pp. 221–45

Nazareth, Peter. 'Conrad's descendants'. *Conradiana* 22.2 (1990), 101–09

Norman, Howard. *'Kiss in the Hotel Joseph Conrad' and Other Stories*. New York: Summit, 1989

Pendleton, Robert. *Graham Greene's Conradian Masterplot*. London: Macmillan, 1995

Peters, Bradley T. 'The significance of dream consciousness in *Heart of Darkness* and *Palace of the Peacock*'. *Conradiana* 22.2 (1990), 127–41

Ross, Stephen. 'Conrad's influence on *Absalom, Absalom!*'. *Studies in American Fiction* 2 (1974), 199–209

Said, Edward. 'Through gringo eyes: with Conrad in Latin America'. *Harper's Magazine*, April 1988, 70–2

Secor, Robert and Debra Moddelmog, comp. *Joseph Conrad and American Writers: A Bibliographical Study of Affinities, Influences, and Relations*. Greenwood, CT: Westport, 1985

Sherry, Norman. *Conrad's Eastern World*. Cambridge: Cambridge University Press, 1966

———. *Conrad's Western World*. Cambridge: Cambridge University Press, 1971

Shklovsky, Viktor. *Theory of Prose*. 1925. Tr. Benjamin Sher. Elmwood Park, IL: Dalkey Archive Press, 1990

Sinyard, Neil. 'Joseph Conrad and Orson Welles'. In *Filming Literature: The Art of Screen Adaptation*. London: Croom Helm, 1986, pp. 111–16

Sutherland, J. G. *At Sea with Joseph Conrad*. 1922. Reprinted Brooklyn: Haskell House, 1971

Szczepaniski, Jan Józef. 'Przypadek'. *Tygodnik powszechny* 4 (1948). Also as 'In Lord Jim's boots'. Tr. Edward Rothert. *Polish Perspectives* 18.1 (1975), 31–44

Turnbull, Andrew, ed. *The Letters of F. Scott Fitzgerald*. New York: Delta, 1965

Wilson, Edmund. *Letters on Literature and Politics, 1912–1972*. Ed. Elena Wilson. New York: Farrar, Straus, Giroux, 1977

Young, Gavin. *In Search of Conrad*. London: Hutchinson, 1991

Zabierowski, Stefan. *Dziedzictwo Conrada w literaturze polskiej XX wieku [The Legacy of Conrad in Twentieth-Century Polish Literature]*. Cracow: Oficyna Literacka, 1992

Works by Joseph Conrad

Almayer's Folly: A Story of an Eastern River, 1895.

An Outcast of the Islands, 1896.

The Nigger of the "Narcissus": A Tale of the Forecastle, 1897.

Tales of Unrest, 1898.

Lord Jim, 1900.

The Inheritors: An Extravagant Story (with Ford Madox Ford), 1901.

Youth: A Narrative, and Two Other Stories, 1902.

Typhoon, 1902.

Romance (with Ford Madox Ford), 1903.

Nostromo: A Tale of the Seaboard, 1904.

The Mirror of the Sea: Memories and Impressions, 1906.

The Secret Agent: A Simple Tale, 1907.

A Set of Six, 1908.

The Point of Honor: A Military Tale, 1908.

Under Western Eyes, 1911.

A Personal Record (Some Reminiscences), 1912.

'Twixt Land and Sea: Tales, 1912.

Chance, 1913.

Victory: An Island Tale, 1915.

Within the Tides: Tales, 1915.

The Shadow-Line: A Confession, 1917.

One Day More, 1917.

"Well Done!," 1918.

Tradition, 1919.

The Arrow of Gold: A Story Between Two Notes, 1919.

The Polish Question: A Note on the Joint Protectorate of the Western Powers and Russia, 1919.

The Shock of War, 1919.

Some Aspects of the Admirable Inquiry into the Loss of the Titanic, 1919.

To Poland in War-Time: A Journey into the East, 1919.

The Tale, 1919.

Prince Roman, 1920.

The Warrior's Soul, 1920.

The Rescue: A Romance of the Shallows, 1920.

Notes on Life and Letters, 1921.

Notes on My Books, 1921.

The Secret Agent, drama, 1921.

The Black Mate, 1922.

The Rover, 1923.

The Nature of a Crime (with Ford Madox Ford), 1924.

Laughing Anne and One Day More: Two Plays, 1924.

Suspense: A Napoleonic Novel, 1925.

Tales of Hearsay, 1925.

Last Essays, Richard Curle, ed., 1926.

Letters to His Wife, 1927.

Letters 1895–1924, Edward Garnett, ed., 1928.

The Sisters, 1928.

Conrad to a Friend: 150 Selected Letters to Richard Curle, Richard Curle, ed., 1928.

Lettres Françaises, Gerard Jean-Aubry, ed., 1929.

Complete Short Stories, 1933.

Annotated Bibliography

Adelman, Gary. *Heart of Darkness: Search for the Unconscious.* Boston: Twayne Publishers, 1987.

Approaching *Heart of Darkness* as one of the first modern, psychological novels, the author analyzes the text and reflects on Conrad's use of symbolism, positing that Marlow's condition is a reflection of Conrad's negative view of imperialism.

Armstrong, Paul B., ed. *Heart of Darkness: A Norton Critical Edition.* 4th ed. New York: W. W. Norton and Company, Inc., 2006.

A valuable all-in-one volume for those becoming acquainted with Conrad and his works, this fourth edition contains the text of the novella, background information, critical essays from Conrad's contemporaries as well as present-day scholars, a chronology, and a bibliography.

Batchelor, John. *The Life of Joseph Conrad: A Critical Biography.* Oxford: Blackwell, 1994.

The author discusses the life of Joseph Conrad, while illuminating important connections between Conrad's life and his writings.

Conrad, Joseph. *Heart of Darkness and The Congo Diary.* London: Penguin, 2007.

Edited by scholars Robert Hampson, Owen Knowles, and J.H. Stape, this edition provides the novella alongside Conrad's *Congo Diary*, revealing the links between Conrad's own experiences in Africa and those represented in *Heart of Darkness*.

———. *Youth; Heart of Darkness; The End of the Tether.* London: Penguin, 1995.

In another Penguin Classics edition, three of Conrad's stories are brought together, with Marlow making an appearance as the narrator of *Youth*, providing further insight into one of Conrad's most famous characters. An introduction by John Lyon examines the ties between the stories.

de Lange, Adriaan M., and Gail Fincham, eds. *Conrad in Africa: New Essays on Heart of Darkness*. New York: Columbia University Press, 2003.

A multidisciplinary collection of essays from a broad range of international scholars, this volume addresses a diverse range of topics including voice, race, and context as they pertain to the novella.

Hawkins, Hunt, and Brian W. Shaffer, eds. *Approaches to Teaching Conrad's Heart of Darkness and The Secret Sharer*. New York: Modern Language Association, 2002.

This book from the Modern Language Association Series, divided into "Materials" and "Approaches," equips teachers with background information and resources, while providing suggestions for addressing in the classroom the challenging controversies that surround the novella.

Knowles, Owen, comp. *An Annotated Critical Bibliography of Joseph Conrad*. New York: St. Martin's Press, 1992.

Conrad scholar Owen Knowles provides a convenient compilation of criticism from 1914 to 1990 with emphasis on post-1970s writings.

Meyers, Jeffrey. *Joseph Conrad: A Biography*. New York: Scribner's, 1991.

Well-known literary biographer Jeffrey Meyers provides new insights into the life of Joseph Conrad in an accessible biography aimed at general readers. Meyers attempts to pinpoint the real-life inspiration behind Conrad's most infamous characters.

Moore, Gene, ed. *Joseph Conrad's Heart of Darkness: A Casebook*. New York: Oxford University Press, 2004.

This casebook presents new material not previously anthologized, including a history of the Congo Free State by Sir Arthur Conan Doyle, memoir excerpts from Conrad's friend, the story *An Outpost of Progress*, along with theoretical exposition reflecting a broad range of approaches.

Murfin, Ross C. *Heart of Darkness: A Case Study in Contemporary Criticism*. New York: Bedford Books of St. Martin's Press, 1989.

Murfin's case study includes a reprint of the 1921 Heinemann edition of *Heart of Darkness* with critical essays commissioned for student readers.

Najder, Zdzisław. *Joseph Conrad: A Life*. Rochester, NY: Camden House, 2007.

In this 2007 work, Najder presents a revised version of his 1983 biography, which received critical praise for being the most complete biography of Conrad available. Najder's Polish heritage and his ability to speak Polish, Russian, French, and English have allowed him to access a significant amount of new material, made available in this revised edition.

Pallua, Ulrich. *Africa's Transition from Colonisation to Independence and Decolonisation: Joseph Conrad's* Heart of Darkness, *Chinua Achebe's* Things Fall Apart, *and Moses Isegawa's* Abyssinian Chronicles. Stuttgart: Ibidem-Verlag, 2004.

Pallua examines Africa's transition from colonization to decolonization utilizing three literary works that represent different points of view and cover three different periods in the continent's history.

Paris, Bernard J. *Conrad's Charlie Marlow: A New Approach to* Heart of Darkness *and* Lord Jim. New York: Palgrave Macmillan, 2005.

The author analyzes Conrad's Marlow within the context of *Heart of Darkness* and *Lord Jim*, revealing a Marlow who is not simply a reflection of Conrad but also a well-conceived, highly developed character.

Said, Edward. *Joseph Conrad and the Fiction of Autobiography*. Cambridge, Mass.: Harvard University Press, 1966.

Although a relatively older work, Said's work focuses on the link between Conrad's own life and his fiction; his thoughts on Western man's difficult adaptation to modernity have influenced Conrad criticism of the last few decades.

Stape, J.H., ed. *The Cambridge Companion to Joseph Conrad*. Cambridge, UK: Cambridge University Press, 1996.

In addition to a chronology of Conrad's life and a detailed list of suggested reading, this companion contains essays on Conrad's major works by an international group of scholars.

Thorburn, David. *Conrad's Romanticism*. New Haven, Conn.: Yale University Press, 1992.

Thorburn's book places Conrad's work within the context of romanticism rather than modernism.

Wake, Paul. *Conrad's Marlow*. Manchester, UK: Manchester University Press, 2008.

This new work provides critical analysis of Conrad's Marlow, examining him from a variety of perspectives including as narrator, character, autobiographical symbol, and messenger.

Watt, Ian. *Conrad in the 19th Century*. Berkeley: University of California Press, 1979.

An extension of Watt's previous scholarship, this volume is commonly regarded as one of the most important critical studies of Joseph Conrad's early works.

Yelton, Donald C. *Mimesis and Metaphor: An Inquiry into the Genesis and Scope of Conrad's Symbolic Imagery*. The Hague, Paris: Mouton, 1967.

The author explores Conrad's use of metaphoric language while acknowledging both the conscious and unconscious forces that play a part in the determination of imagery and symbol.

Contributors

Harold Bloom is Sterling Professor of the Humanities at Yale University. He is the author of 30 books, including *Shelley's Mythmaking*, *The Visionary Company*, *Blake's Apocalypse*, *Yeats*, *A Map of Misreading*, *Kabbalah and Criticism*, *Agon: Toward a Theory of Revisionism*, *The American Religion*, *The Western Canon*, and *Omens of Millennium: The Gnosis of Angels, Dreams, and Resurrection*. *The Anxiety of Influence* sets forth Professor Bloom's provocative theory of the literary relationships between the great writers and their predecessors. His most recent books include *Shakespeare: The Invention of the Human*, a 1998 National Book Award finalist, *How to Read and Why*, *Genius: A Mosaic of One Hundred Exemplary Creative Minds*, *Hamlet: Poem Unlimited*, *Where Shall Wisdom Be Found?*, and *Jesus and Yahweh: The Names Divine*. In 1999, Professor Bloom received the prestigious American Academy of Arts and Letters Gold Medal for Criticism. He has also received the International Prize of Catalonia, the Alfonso Reyes Prize of Mexico, and the Hans Christian Andersen Bicentennial Prize of Denmark.

Zdzisław Nadjer is a literary historian and an authority on the works of Joseph Conrad. He is the author of *Conrad Under Familial Eyes* and *Joseph Conrad: A Chronicle*. He has served as president of the Joseph Conrad Society of Poland since 1993 and has taught at Warsaw University as well as at many American universities.

Peter Edgerly Firchow is professor of English at the University of Minnesota. He is the author of *Envisioning Africa: Racism and Imperialism in Conrad's Heart of Darkness* as well as many other book-length critical studies of literature.

Albert J. Guerard was a novelist, teacher, and critic. A professor emeritus of English at Stanford University, he was the author of *Conrad the Novelist* published by Harvard University Press and Oxford University Press as well as numerous other works.

Jakob Lothe is professor of literature at the University of Oslo. He is the author of *Conrad's Narrative Method* and *Narrative in Fiction and Film: An Introduction*. Lothe is also one of the editors of *Joseph Conrad: Voice, Sequence, History, Genre*.

Ford Madox Ford was a novelist, poet, editor, and critic. He was the founder of *The English Review* and *The Transatlantic Review*, widely recognized for their impact on modern literature. Ford collaborated with Joseph Conrad on two novels.

Martin Tucker is faculty emeritus at the C. W. Post campus of Long Island University. Tucker has edited more than twenty volumes of literary encyclopedias. He is also the author of many critical studies including *Joseph Conrad, Africa in Modern Literature*, and *Literary Exile in the Twentieth Century*.

Cedric T. Watts is professor of English at the University of Sussex. He is the author and editor of many literary texts including *The Deceptive Texts: An Introduction to Covert Plots* and *Joseph Conrad: A Literary Life*. He has written extensively on the works of Conrad.

Mark Wollaeger teaches English at Vanderbilt University. In addition to authoring *Joseph Conrad and the Fictions of Skepticism* and *Modernism, Media & Propaganda: British Narrative from 1900 to 1945*, he has written widely on other topics related to modernist literature. Wollaeger is the co-editor of Modernist Literature and Culture, a book series from Oxford University Press.

Daniel C. Melnick is professor emeritus of English at Cleveland State University. He is the author of "Under Western Eyes and Silence" and *Fullness of Dissonance: Modern Fiction and the Aesthetics of Music*.

Chinua Achebe, author of the celebrated novel *Things Fall Apart*, is also a poet, teacher, and critic. His critical essay "An Image of Africa: Racism in Conrad's Heart of Darkness" has influenced several decades of Conrad criticism. He is the Charles P. Stevenson, Jr. Professor of Languages and Literature at Bard College.

Lissa Schneider is the author of *Conrad's Narratives of Difference: Not Exactly Tales for Boys* as well as several articles pertaining to the study of Conrad. In 2007, Schneider received the Bruce Harkness Young Conrad Scholar Award. She teaches English at the University of Wisconsin-River Falls.

Marvin Mudrick was professor of English at the University of California, Santa Barbara. He was the editor of Prentice Hall's *Conrad: A Collection of Critical Essays*.

Gene M. Moore is the editor of *Joseph Conrad's Heart of Darkness: A Casebook* from Oxford University Press and *Conrad on Film*, among other works. He is senior lecturer in English at the University of Amsterdam.

Acknowledgments

Zdzisław Nadjer, "Conrad in His Historical Perspective." From *Critical Essays on Joseph Conrad* by Ted Billy, pp. 19–22, 26–28. Copyright © 1987 by Ted Billy. Reprinted with permission.

Peter Edgerly Firchow, "Envisioning Kurtz." From *Envisioning Africa: Racism and Imperialism in Conrad's* Heart of Darkness, pp. 62–63, 65–68, 208–212. Copyright © 2000 by the University Press of Kentucky. Reprinted with permission.

Albert J. Guerard, "The Journey Within." From *Joseph Conrad: Heart of Darkness*, pp. 326, 328–330, 334–336. Copyright © 2006 by W. W. Norton & Company. Reprinted with permission.

Jakob Lothe, "Conradian Narrative." From *The Cambridge Companion to Joseph Conrad*, pp. 165–169, 176–178. Copyright © 1996. Reprinted with the permission of Cambridge University Press.

Ford Madox Ford, "Conrad on the Theory of Fiction." From *Conrad: A Collection of Critical Essays*, edited by Marvin Mudrick, pp. 172–174. Copyright © 1924 by Ford Madox Ford. Book copyright © 1966 by Prentice-Hall, Inc. Reprinted by permission.

Martin Tucker, "The Dream-Nightmare: *Heart of Darkness*." From *Joseph Conrad*, pp. 31–34. Copyright © 1976 by Frederick Ungar Publishing Co. Reprinted with permission.

Cedric T. Watts, "Conrad's Covert Plots and Transtextual Narratives." From *Critical Essays on Joseph Conrad* by Ted Billy, pp. 67, 70–71. Copyright © 1987 by Ted Billy. Reprinted with permission.

Mark A. Wollaeger, "'Heart of Darkness': Visionary Skepticism." From *Joseph Conrad and the Fictions of Skepticism*, pp. 67–73, 214–215. Copyright © 1990 by the Board of Trustees of the Leland Stanford Jr. University.

Every effort has been made to contact the owners of copyrighted material and secure copyright permission. Articles appearing in this volume generally appear much as they did in their original publication with few or no editorial changes. In some cases, foreign language text has been removed from the original essay. Those interested in locating the original source will find the information cited above.

Index

Characters in literary works are indexed by first name (if any), followed by the name of the work in parentheses